Fine Wine, Guns and Angels

Fine Wine, Guns and Angels

The Extraordinary Life of Chris Constantino

Chris Constantino

Copyright © 2023 by Chris Constantino

All rights reserved. No part of this book may be reproduced or used in any manner without written permission of the copyright owner except for the use of quotations in a book review.

For more information contact: constantino71@gmx.com

Revised edition July 2023

Introduction

This is <u>Not</u> Based on a True Story – This <u>IS</u> a True Story

My name is Chris Constantino. I was formerly known as Spyros Constantinos. I was born in Hackney in East London in August 1971. My parents came to England from Cyprus with their parents in the 1950s and both settled in the Archway area of North London. They got married in 1969 and I was born in 1971.

My life has never been ordinary but since I was 14 years old, no-one could have imagined the life that I have lived since then. While you read through my book I want you to imagine the following:

- That by the time I was 7, I had been kidnapped, been witness to an Armed Robbery at my mums shop, witnessed my mum almost die in a car accident and that I was probably only seconds away from drowning while on holiday

- Losing both my parents in a tragic car accident at 14 years old which is what happened to me.

- Being badly injured my-self in the accident including a broken leg, burns, broken ribs and fractured skull.

- That I was kept in a coma for 2 weeks after the accident, with the initial thoughts of the Doctors being that I would not survive.

- In my late teens I started to believe I was the son of a superior alien colony that was sent to earth to help the world free itself of poverty.

- At a later stage in life being diagnosed with Bi Polar disorder including Psychosis which was almost certainly developed from the car accident.

- Living in Los Angeles for a while in 1991 with some very interesting and funny stories.

- Being a top salesman where I done things my way and became a legend within the Timeshare Industry.

- Living the life of a Holiday rep on the Greek Island of Corfu

- Turning over millions of pounds in complex investment schemes that ultimately failed due to me being defrauded whilst living in Marbella in Spain and losing millions of pounds for myself and my clients.

- Being involved with gangsters whilst in Spain, playing Russian roulette, being in the middle of 3 shootings where one of the bullets in one of the shootings just missed me.

- Being involved in some of the wildest parties you will have ever heard of whilst living in Marbella including my experience of being at a party on a £300m yacht.

- Meeting many celebrities while living in Marbella.

- Having, alcohol, drugs and sex addiction.

- My incredible memoirs of being in prison for 4 years, being amongst suicide attempts which included myself, drug abuse, the spice drug causing scenes that you would expect to see in a horror film, fights, racism, mental torture and much more.

- Having visits that I believe have in effect been proven to have taken place by superior alien beings (The 3 Angels) that have guided me to writing this book and re-sending the message from some of the prophecies from the ancient scriptures to you in a more simple form.

- 500 Shades of Sex – you will just have to read this chapter!!

- Multiple incidents where it appears the manic episodes I suffer with in my Bi Polar Disorder caused me to act very strangely.

- My on-going legal battle against 'Corruption within the UK Justice System' including my triumph of hope and persistence over overwhelming odds.

- Many other aspects of my life that include, my love of Tottenham Hotspur Football Club, messages from superior beings that can change the world, Free Will, God, Homosexuality, Remorse, My Life now, Curing poverty and my End Game.

Early days

Hand of God

I was 5 years old. My grandmother's sister was deeply unwell and hospitalised. We were going to visit her on this particular day. As soon as I learned of this I remember having this overwhelming feeling that once I touched her arm or held her hand she would feel much better and recover. This wasn't a feeling of 'oh because she loves me and by seeing me it will make her feel happier or better' it was a feeling that I had the powers to heel her…I couldn't wait to get there and with the powers that I thought were within me I could completely make her better…I don't recall what happened after that but I often wonder why I had such a feeling and at 5 years old… it was overwhelmingly powerful. The reason I start my memoirs with this fact is that this overwhelming feeling as described has continued to exist within my life for various reasons and you will read how I have had close encounters with Angels that I have evidenced to you

Mum

My mum was a bubbly character. She was a good looking lady that liked to be the life and soul of the party. It's funny… when I use to go to her hairdressers in school holidays in Dalston – East London where she owned the shop, she never wanted me to call her mum as it made her feel old. I use to call her Den which is short for Denise the English version of her actual Greek name which was DESPINA.

Dad

My dad was the opposite 6ft 1inches tall… very muscular and barely an ounce of fat on him. He was very laid back and quite quiet. He was a good man that never harmed or offended anybody. He was an electrician but could do everything in the building trade from plumbing to carpentry to flooring, tiling … he was also halfway through building an extension to our house by himself … unfortunate he never got to finish it as that's when the accident happened.

I am a complete split between both my parents in looks, physique and personality wise.

Cyprus

Now most of my family originate from a small village in the Troodos mountain's in Cyprus called Dora. If you go back 100 years there were probably only around 200 people living there.

After the Second World War mainly in the 1950s, as Cyprus was part of the British Commonwealth, Greek Cypriots were invited over to come and live in the UK as part of a rebuilding programme…Cyprus wasn't a major tourist destination back then as it is now so there was very little money about.

Many Cypriots took the invitation and moved to the UK ... mainly to North London.

Now over the years stemming from that small population that came from our village in Cyprus it is quite amazing to see the contrast of lives that have existed from those that came to live in the UK after the War.

This small village has ultimately produced within the UK several multi-millionaires and a couple of relatives that have made money in the hundreds of millions. There has also been persons that have originated from this small village tin Cyprus hat have been involved in suicides and murders amongst other things... I don't know why... just the way it is.

I as many other people do have a theory on Cyprus. If you look where it is geographically it is pretty much the centre of the world... why, we'll just a few miles further to the east you have the start of the Middle east, including Israel and the Arab world... just a few miles to the north across the sea is Turkey which is an Islamic country but with an element of western civilisation. A few miles to the South you have Africa and the finally across the Mediterranean sea to the West is the entrance to Europe... try and think of another place in the world that is more central to so many continents and races as Cyprus is... There isn't one.

So over the years travellers from all areas surrounding Cyprus have travelled there and settled. Now thinking of the intermingling of these races on the island of Cyprus spanning hundreds of years... us Cypriots must have the most diverse historic blood lines in the world!

Armed Robbery 1977

I use to spend most school holidays at my mum's hairdressing salon on Kingsland road in Hackney. It was and still is one of the toughest areas in the whole of England.

During those School holidays I use to spend most of the day roaming the Kingsland road looking at shops. There was a toy shop about 100 metres from my mums shop. I use to spend at least an hour of the day staring through the shop window and admiring the toys.

There was one time when my mums shop was robbed by 3 guys. They came in with knives welding and robbed the till. As they were robbing the shop I walked in from the street. My mum shouted to me to go back out and come back in a little while. I think I was only around 6 years old but could see that something was clearly wrong. I looked at one of the robbers and he nodded his head in sort of affirmation that I should leave.

For some reason I remember going straight to the cafe and buying myself a cheese roll that cost 5p! I sat down to eat my cheese roll. A couple of minutes in, a couple of the other shop owners along the road saw me and said hello. "How's your mum Spyros"… they said.

"She's ok" I remember saying

But then I followed onto to say "but there are some men in the shop holding knives"…. The lady who was part of the couple started asking me questions …. Whilst the man immediately got up and left the cafe…obviously he was going to my mum's shop to see what was going on.

The robbers had left by the time he got there…my mums shop was robbed but no one was hurt. This was my first experience of criminal activity. However the event although very serious seemed to pass me bye as is it was a nothing. However this was merely a drop in the ocean compared to what I would be in the middle of 'Crime Wise' for much of the rest of my life!

The usual questions

Whenever my mum picked me up from school or we drove back home from her hairdressers in Hackney I always had 3 questions for her?

What's for dinner tonight mum?

What's on TV tonight mum?

Are we going out anywhere tonight mum?

Standard procedure without fail!

From a young age I was always looking forward to or seeking that next bit of pleasure. Those 3 things that I asked my mum could sway my happiness at that moment in time.

There were 2 things that I liked to hear the most within my mum's response.

Either we were going around to one of my cousin's house which meant great play time or going out to eat.

My favourite food

If we were going out to eat, this would usually be Scorpios Greek restaurant in Tottenham. I loved it there. We always used to get a Meze… this is around 20 or 30 Greek dishes mainly on small plates. Meats, fish, salad, rice, chips, dips… fucking loved it…I was a slim child until I was about 7 but going to Scorpios I believe was one of the triggers to put on weight and have spent most of my life since being a fatty lol! – However my late granddad was always overweight also and he lived until 105 years old! – I will let you into his secret later.

Drowning & Running Away From Home – 1977 – well almost!

From birth until I was about 2 years old we lived above my mums shop In Hackney. From the ages of 2 to 10 I lived on the North Circular Road in Palmers Green which is in North London. This is a busy road like a main road an 'A' road. I don't know why my parents bought a house exactly there! …. We lived right next to a brook which I almost fell into once when riding my bike… I lost control and got stuck on the edge to about a 10ft drop into the brook which was next to our house – I was screaming out for ages until someone heard me. I was struggling to keep my balance on the edge. I was saved in time. Had I have fallen down and into the brook I may have drowned as the water was high that day. It was very close.

Drowning seems to have become a bit of a theme in my story as you will see.

Running Away!

One time around this period, I remember getting into an argument with my mum. I told her I was going to run away…

"Go on then" she said which I found strange, she probably knew that I wouldn't lol! So I set off on my bike along the pavement and continued down the North Circular Road where it met the cross junction with Green Lanes. I stopped, pondered for a while then rode my bicycle back home.

"I thought you were running away" my mum said

"I was" I said

"So why have you come back" she said…

"So, I got to Green Lanes and then remembered" I said

"Remembered what" she said

"That I'm not allowed to cross the road"….

She burst out laughing and couldn't wait to tell her sister on the phone. She used to take the piss out of me for years to come for what happened.

There were a fair few other incidents involving myself and family members as a child. There were 2 suicides where relatives shot themselves in the head, murders, stealing, accidents, heart attacks at a young age, strokes, diabetes, fires, burglaries, kidnapping, being held up by armed robbers as you have already read and more.

However the scariest time I remember as a child was when my Mum drove through a shop window - I was very young, I'm guessing I was about 6 or 7 years old. My dad drove me to my godparents up the road… close family would be gathering around. Something serious had happened. My mum had been driving home from work as usual, going down the Kingsland Road towards Stoke Newington. A car was heading towards her but on the wrong side of the road… she veered off to the left and off the road and drove straight into a shop smashing through the shop window. She was quite badly hurt. My grandmother (my mum's mother) was also around my godparents.

She was screaming out in Greek "My daughter, my daughter". It was peak, very bad. Everyone was waiting to hear from my dad who went to the hospital to see what had happened and how my mum was.

Due to the smashing glass she had been cut up quite badly. I was too young to understand for sure what was going on. I know she stayed in hospital for a few days but ultimately she was fine although she did have scaring around her face and body.

Kidnapped in 1978

The next most frightening moment was when I was kidnapped. I met with a couple of older lads who hung around the Kingsland Road. This was back in the 1970s so people were less cautious then of their kids hanging around the streets. The group of us lads went to one of the boy's houses… he had some new games so we went there to check them out. I believe that I must have been around 7 years old at the time. We were in the flats just behind Kingsland Road. It was getting late and I was aware that I should be heading back to my mums shop as she would be finishing soon. However, the other boys decided not to let me go… I told them I had to as my mum would be looking for me. I was in effect kidnapped and forced to stay there for at least two hours after the time my mum would have finished work.

I sat there not knowing what to do. I didn't know when they were going to let me go. There were no parents around – maybe out at work – I don't know – what the fuck was I to do. I knew my mum would be worrying. I just sat there for ages with the boys not paying much attention to me. I kept reminding them I had to go and at one stage started crying. They just took the piss out of me. I then started to get angry.

Then one of the little fuckers had a bright idea! Not…"Let's cut his hair off" one of them said. Another boy goes to the other room and comes back with a pair of kitchen scissors.

"Oh shit" I thought! They teased me for a while about how they were going to cut my hair off. I stood up and put my back against the wall. I didn't know what to do.

One of the boys approaches me with the scissors and another holds me against the wall. There were 3 of the little cunts. They were all a couple of years older than me. My arms and back were pinned against the wall. The scissors were raised above my head. I heard a couple of snips then I fucking lost it. I got one of my arms loose and raised it to my head. I felt the scissors and grabbed them. I immediately started waving the scissors about making jab moves with the scissors towards the boys. I swear I was going to stab one of them. The boys shit themselves.

"I want to get out" I shouted. One of the boys moved towards the front door and opened it. I remember they had their hands up in the air like I was pointing a gun at them. I ran out… down the flight of stairs and back towards Kingsland road. I threw the scissors in the street.

The boys thought it was funny - well it fucking wasn't. It was dark, I was fuming and started heading back down Kingsland Road towards the shop. I looked up and I saw my mum. She was crying. She saw me and started to scream. She was whacking me and cuddling me at the same time. There was a police car parked on the pavement right outside her shop and the blue light was flashing. She spoke with the cops for a while. I was crying, shitting myself, I knew I was in big trouble. However it weren't my bloody fault. Soon we set off to go home…. Mum is still crying… "Just you wait until you get home"… that meant dealing with my dad…. I have no recollection of what happened when we got home… but I believe once I explained what had happened it calmed the situation down.

Trauma

I believe that this 'kidnapping' incident caused me temporary trauma. I don't know for how long the following went on for but I reckon it was a good couple of months.

I would grab some hair strands from my head and then twist them around and then somehow tie the strands into a little knot. I would then pull that knotted bunch of strands out. I was literally pulling my hair out. I think the condition is called trichotillomania……it was like I had some kind of nervous edge and to calm myself I needed to pull my hair out… what a fucked up situation that was.

However what was equally as bad if not worse was at the same time I found myself a new hobby. Unfortunately this was the mass murder of ants! What the fuck!

It was summertime. Towards the front of the garden and by the first pond there was a concrete slab patio area. One of the slabs had cracked through age leaving a space underneath it. This space was infiltrated by a large army of ants. There were hundreds and hundreds of them. I sat on the bench next to the nest of ants and I would watch them for a while. They were scurrying around but for the most part it looked like their movements had purpose. They were organised and each seem to have its own job to do. I found it fascinating.

For some fucked up reason I decided to disrupt their flow of organisation. I would stamp on a few of them… basically kill them and see how the other ants would react…. I could see different patterns and formations being displayed. It didn't matter how many I killed they would somehow and almost instantly regroup in a new structured way.

After a while I got bored and decided just to kill them all. I would literally sit there until there were none left alive. Where I believed that there were some hiding in cracks and crevices I would wait them out until I got them.

When I look back upon this now I think how fucking awful. What possessed a 7 year old boy to do such a thing. It's a little worrying actually. Well that was 45 years ago. I can't explain what was going through my mind then.

Drowning In Corfu around 1978

Drowning in Corfu - I recon I must have been 6 or 7 years old. We were on holiday on the Greek Island of Corfu. I entered the sea by some rocks…. I jumped into the sea. Now I can't remember categorically if I was able to swim at that age but I am 99% sure that I would have been. The sea must have been deeper than I thought. There was no one else around. I couldn't keep myself afloat …. I was going under … fighting my way up then back down… screaming for my life… I don't remember how the fuck I got into that situation as I just said.

I'm sure I could swim… but I can't recall what the problem was…why was I drowning?, it seemed to go on for ages… I was struggling, I swallowed some water…was I going to die…I see a man standing on one of the rocks, he jumps in and pull's me out…my dad appears and realised what had happened… I don't know exactly what happened after that but it never stopped me going back in the sea. However had that man not appeared for another minute that would have probably been the end of me. That was my second close to death experience, but that was just the beginning of a life that has been filled with numerous close to death experiences as you will see.

Later that day, I remember meeting up with a friend that I had met on the holiday. I was explaining to him what had happened whilst we were playing mini golf. It appears in my hand motions of explaining the drowning incident; I was also waving the golf club about. I accidentally hit my mate with the golf club I was holding right in the eye. I must have cut him bad. Blood was spurting out everywhere… poor kid! Fuck me what a disastrous day!

Birth of My Sister - Rebecca

My sister Rebecca was born in June 1980. I think initially that my parents only wanted to have one child. This was for the main part because they both worked full time and they had bad experiences with me when I was a baby in regards to being left with a baby sitter. I would always scream and shout when my mum left me with a babysitter. This as you would imagine caused her a lot of stress and made her working day even more difficult than what it already was.

So at around 7am my cousin George and I were woken with the news that my mum had given birth to a girl. We celebrated the birth of my sister by jumping up and down on the bed. I had waited a long time for a brother or sister! I'm not sure that I knew any other kid that didn't have siblings… it was good for me.

Although there is a 9 year age gap between us it was still better than being a single child.

Cousin George - Murder

I was always close with my cousin George growing up. As just stated, he was there with me that morning at the birth of my baby sister. I am just a few months older than him. We spent much of our youth together.

However when he was 12 in 1983 he his mum and dad moved back to Cyprus. I used to see him every couple of years on holidays.

The problem is that George, although a bright guy always had a bit of a screw loose for want of a better phrase. When we were about 16 there were about 8 of us cousins congregated at his house for the day. The parents of the different cousins were all out for the day… so it was left to us cousins to form our own entertainment. I don't know what set George off but he started throwing furnishings from the upstairs of the house onto the street below via the balcony… it was crazy… you see he had crazy moments like these and no one really knew why.

Around 20 years ago or so George was up staying in Liverpool with his girlfriend at the time. They soon after had a son together.

On one particular occasion he was with his girlfriend and they were around his girlfriend's auntie's house. Her auntie's boyfriend was also there with her. Anyway they were all seated around the living room having a chit chat when George made a remark that the auntie had appeared to have put on a bit of weight. The auntie's boyfriend took offence to this remark and he and George started arguing. The arguing continued out onto the street… George ran back inside picked up a knife and as they wrestled on the floor, George stabbed the guy to death.

George received a life sentence but I believe only served 14 years. George lives in Cyprus and is never allowed to leave the country. Unfortunately for him his mental health has suffered a lot over the years.

Junior School

So my sister had finally arrived. At this time I was in Junior School. I loved junior school. It was a good time for me. I enjoyed all of the activities that you do at that age basically from 7 years old until 11 years old. No stresses or too much homework… lots of play time. I use to love the 'Bring and Buy sales that happened every year. There would be prize draws, games, competitions and various other goods that you could buy that had been brought in by other kids.

This was the time that I really started getting into football and 'Match' magazine. I would scour the stalls and look for anything football related. For me this was the equivalent to the buzz when women go out shoe shopping! lol..When I was about 7 and in Junior School I was in the School football team but unfortunately by the time I was about 8 or 9 I was getting too overweight to be able to run like the other kids so had to drop out of playing – too much fatty Greek food – Funny story with regards my weight – at around this age I use to go and stay around my grandmothers in the flats in Edmonton once a week on a Friday night after school.

She would have a big plate of food ready for me:

GRAN – There you go Spyro – your favourite food
ME – Wow that's a lot Yiayia (Greek word for Gran)
GRAN – Eat it all
ME – I will

.....after I have finished
GRAN – you eat too much – you are getting fat
ME – You told me to eat it all

Later that evening.......
GRAN – Do you want cake?
ME – I'm full Yiayia
GRAN – Don't be silly a little more won't harm you!!

That was a typical weekly conversation – I couldn't win – I was destined to become a fat boy! lol

Greek Island of Kos around 1981 or 1982 – Octopus and Jellyfish

I think my most memorable holiday as a child was when I was about 10, so my sister would have been a baby maybe 1 or 2 years old. We were on a 2 week holiday on the Greek island of Kos.

We were staying in apartment's right by the sea. On the patch of beach we frequented there was a restaurant that we had lunch and dinner at on most days.

This is when I discovered snorkelling. There were plenty of fish to look at. I absolutely loved it. I would snorkel for ages and ages at a time. I also had a fish net .... You know one of those ones with a round ended rim and small net at the end of a long wooden pole.

Now I don't know what these particular fish were called but they were ugly buggers. They swam right at the bottom just over the sand. That would make them the easiest to catch as all you needed to do was hover the net over them when they sat still for a minute, then force the net down over them and into the sand. Then scoop the net upwards… there you go… got one.

The fish would be put into a small bucket of water…. I would show off my catch to my mum and dad then a little while later put the fish back in the sea. It's funny I remember catching 39 fish on the holiday… I don't know how or I why I remember that…. Just one of those things I suppose!

But those fish weren't to be my biggest catch! So the local kids, mostly around my age, would often go into the sea with spear guns… I wasn't sure what they were trying to catch at first and I'm not sure I remember them ever catching anything of any significance.

Anyway I was out in the sea doing my usual daily snorkelling and I approached the rocky area as I would often do…Oh my God… I couldn't fucking believe it. There was a small Octopus spread over a rock. I say small but things look bigger in the water and at first sight to me it looked big.

I stopped moving. Just like all fish the octopus could have shot off with any sudden movement. I looked at it for a while… "I've got to get it" I thought. I only had my small net… I had to give it a go though.

I stayed still for a little longer… the little bugger wasn't moving… good…I slowly moved myself sideways on and stretched my arm out with the net pole in hand. I slowly moved the net towards the Octopus… "Please don't move"….I thought. I then surged at it with the net… I've bloody got it. The net was now covering most of the Octopus which I had trapped against the rock… I scooped it out….now holding the pole with 2 hands and out of the water I shouted – "Dad..dad", 'I've got an Octopus'… he got up and started walking towards me and he turns round and shouts to my mum to come over… they couldn't believe it, nor could I… my dad found a large container and we quickly filled it with water… in went the Octopus… others on the beach also came over including the local kids with their spear guns… I was like the star of the show lol!

The local boys wanted to take it to the restaurant as a 'catch of the day' as such… but I wasn't having it… after a while I just wanted to put it back in the sea which I did…. However had that been now, I would have taken it straight to the restaurant and have them cook it up for me! I love a bit of Octopus… you should try it if you haven't done so already.

However 'Octopus gate' was not the last of the dramas on this particular holiday.

So once again I'm in the sea and near the rocky area where I had previously found the octopus… whilst doing my usual thing I felt something very soft and light wrap itself in a spiral way round my leg….. A few seconds later I'm screaming my head off…"Aaaahhh…. Aaaahhhh"…'Dad.. dad'… He looks over at me and was probably thinking what the fuck was going on! I'm still screaming… dad runs into the water…. He picks me up and walks me to the sand.

I had been stung by a jellyfish. Wow that is fucking painful! There was a big thick bulging mark spirally running down my leg. I was in agony…

It was a couple of days before I could go back in the sea… gutted… but it didn't scare me off.

I think it was that particular holiday that made me fall in love with the sea… in fact being in crystal clear water with some fish life roaming around is one of the best feelings in the world that I have ever experienced.

Early senior school years
1983 to 1985

There are a few things I remember about this time. The girls would dress like the pop stars of the early 1980's – Adam and the Ants – Boy George –Duran Duran etc. Great music was coming out of the UK back then. The boys were into the Panini football sticker albums. Any spare cash I had at the time would be spent on the stickers. I didn't enjoy senior school as much as junior school. In fact I found many of the lessons boring. I was an above average student but I found I could only concentrate on subjects or topics that I was interested in. If not, my mind would wander onto other things like football or girls.

One of the highlights of those early years was when I bought sex magazines for the first time lol!....

I was at school- Minchenden Lower School in the Southgate/ Winchmore Hill area of North London. I would have been around 12 or 13 years old. The word got round that there were a couple of lads from the year above selling sex magazines. I was coming of that age if you know what I mean… I needed to get some - a couple of my mates and I got our money together… met up with the older boys… and completed our transaction. I bought 2 magazines. Walking home I was so excited… I couldn't wait to get home and check them out.… As any heterosexual male… I wasn't disappointed lol!!.

There was this one time I threw a stick at my mate 'Milti' and it stuck in his head!. On this occasion at around 12 years old we were out on the school field. Milti and I were having an argument about something. We walked apart… we must have been 30ft apart… Milti shouted out something at me. I picked up a long stick … a piece of tree branch/twig. I threw it at Milti… incredibly it hit him on the forehead and struck there… what are the fucking odds on that. He pulled it out… nothing serious luckily… we had a fight which was more like a wrestling match… I weighed twice as much as him… I sat on him… and that was that I suppose.

House Burglary

When we were about 13 years old there was a steady group of mates that ultimately stayed in touch as a whole until our late thirties to early forties until we slowly went our own way..

At age of 13 we all got into cycling. That was the time when the BMX bike's came out which was in the early 1980's. However after spending ages deciding on which BMX bike we would buy, we ultimately decided to buy racing bikes as we were more interested in long distance cycling rather than showboating!

What was really strange that at an evening around my auntie's house at that time, there were 2 main subjects of conversation. The first was as just mentioned which bicycle I should get and the second one was a long discussion about home burglaries. I have no factual recollection of why that was such a profound subject of conversation that evening other than maybe it was to do with footsteps that had been found in the snow in her back garden that morning.

So here's the strange thing. When we got back home that night from the visit we discovered that our house had been fucking burgled. What are the chances of that!! I was about 12 or 13 at the time so it was more of an exciting thing than a big deal to me but not for my mum. She was in tears. The house has been ransacked. It wasn't the first time though. I remember being burgled at our previous home on 2 other previous occasions. The police were called round. The burglars had entered the house by the double glazing doors at the back. They would have climbed over the fence at the back of our garden. This led to a very, very small alleyway to the road next to us. Scummy fuckers! I don't know what they took but at that age I didn't really give a shit either.

Planet of the Apes

It was 1983 and I would have been around 12 and my sister 3 years old. We were at London Zoo with our parents.

Apes and Monkeys had always been my favourite animals and I was exited about seeing them in real life.

My sister and I proceeded to the Apes section whilst my mum and dad finished their drinks.

We could see the Ape enclosure just ahead of us. As my sister and I approached, I noticed that one of the Apes… it looked like a silver back… fucking massive, suddenly stood on its back feet, just behind the glass and was looking in our direction.

The Ape started screaming and banging it's chest. We got closer and closer. It was clear that this super huge Ape was looking at me... we slowed down in curiosity. The Ape starting banging the glass.

We were there, right in front of the Silver Back. He was looking at me. Right into my eyes. He stopped banging the glass and calmed down. There were people standing around looking at me and the Ape... they must have thought 'what the fuck is going on'.

My sister stood still and I approached the glass. Other apes from the enclosure were hurriedly moving towards us. They were all screaming and jumping.

I was now right in front of the glass. The Silver Back pressed his face on the glass. For some reason I did the same. Our faces were almost touching. There was just 1 or 2 inches of glass between us.

We were looking right into each others eyes. I seem to remember his eyes were green.

Tears started rolling down from the apes eyes. I felt something so profoundly emotional at this time I cannot even begin to explain.

I was close to tears. Something was happening between us. The ape somehow knew something about me. He was trying to tell me something.

It was overwhelming. I don't know how long this moment lasted. I was surrounded by people that were watching what was happening.

After a short while, I moved away and grabbed my sisters hand and walked back to my parents. As we walked along I looked back and there must have been 20 or 30 people staring at me.

What happened that day will live with me and my sister forever. It was special but I do wonder what it was about me that made the apes react as they did.

Was there something about me that was special to them or could they see something in me that they found so profound.

I'm not sure I will ever know.

Stand By Me

So we now had our racer bicycles. We often used to ride out to Hertfordshire which is a county just North of London. This one time we stopped at a large Barn in the middle of nowhere which was packed with hay stacks. Good place to have a jump around we thought.

There was no-one around to tell us off – it was very remote. It was all going well until I found a rotting human skeleton hidden within the hay stacks.

"Fucking hell"… 'look at this' I Shouted.

For the first few minutes it was intriguing but then someone started speaking about murder and if the killer could see us there he would have to kill us.

"Someone's been fucking murdered" My mate Aydin replies.

We suddenly panicked and shit ourselves and shot off on our bikes.

It was the 1984 FA Cup Final day. It was Watford v Everton - so we were speeding off from the barn… we were probably 20 miles from home and it was pissing down with rain… although it was a summers kind of day to start with the rain hitting our hands felt really cold… my hands were going numb after a while. Some of us were faster cyclists than the others… Every few miles the front man would stop so the others could catch up then start again…

it was getting painful…and the hammering rain was slowing us down… I wanted to get back in time for the cup final…

We made it back soaking wet and knackered…. We stopped off at the Green in Southgate which was like a central point for us. We were all going to head our own way home back from there.

"What about the skeleton" I said – Everyone just looked at me.

"Ok we don't say anything for the moment" – 'we need to think about it' I said.

"If we call the police they might think it was something to do with us". I said.

Anyway it was too rainy to stand around fucking about… we all went home…nothing much more was ever really spoken again amongst us about what we had seen that day… I'm pretty sure none of us told anyone… we were 13 years old and really not sure about the whole thing. I do sometimes wonder though who that skeleton of a person was and how they ended up getting there. It can't have been for good reasons… we should have told the police… yeah we really should. It makes me feel bad when I think about it now.

We never told anyone… I don't know why… I suppose that was our 'stand by me' moment but not for good reasons – only that we were scared we would be somehow blamed.

Starting off smoking a pipe then cigars

When we were about 13 years one of my mates bought a smoking pipe… so we all bought one lol!! So we smoked pipes for a year, then we went to cigars for a year and then finally onto cigarettes by the age of 15 - a bit unusual but that's we did!

Can you imagine a group of 13 year old lads gathered together, maybe sitting in a park on a summer's day smoking pipes. We use to take our pipes to school and go to the back of the field during break in a small forested area where no one could see us and pipe away. We would stink of tobacco. We were sometimes asked by teachers why we stunk of tobacco but we would just smile at them and say that we didn't know – what else could we have said! lol.

The cigar smell was even stronger, so after a while we thought that it would be best to do the right thing and smoke cigarettes instead! Lol

The New One Pound Coin

Around this time the One pound coin was released for the first time. My mates and I didn't have access to lot of money…. One of us came up with the bright idea of gluing 2 x one Pence pieces together which form the approximate thickness of a £1 coin although the circumference was still smaller and then painting the 2 glued together coins in gold colour.

There you go - we had a £1 coin. One of us… I can't remember who, was given the duty of trying to use the coin in the local newsagents. It worked… they came out with a packet of 10 Rothmans cigarettes and some chocolate. What a result we thought. We believed that we were some kind of clever enterprising gangsters lol… but we realised we got lucky and would be a good idea not to try it again.

Although we didn't do it again, the word had somehow spread to other schools in the North London area. There were kids all over the place making fake £1 coins. It got into the local newspaper or news. Shops were warned off by what was happening. It only lasted a month or so….oh dear….whoops ..I'm sorry for the part I played in that….!

The accident – 27th July 1986 – My Life Changes Forever

We were going on a family holiday to Greece. However on this occasion we were going to drive there instead of flying. It was going to take around 3 days. I had 2 sets of uncles also coming in their cars with 2 children (my cousins) in each. So there were 3 cars and 12 people in total – 6 adults and 6 children

We set off from London earlier this day. I was very excited about this holiday. By now I was a total sea lover and I would have 5 of my cousins with me. Happy days……

The last thing I remember was being on the German and Belgium border late at night. We stopped off at a late night coffee bar. I ate a donut… then that's it.

Shortly afterwards my life would change forever. The only reason we know what happened in all likeliness is because my uncles were driving in the cars behind ours with their families.

Powering along a German autobahn my dad it would appear in all likelihood fell asleep at the wheel. The car suddenly veered to the right and smashed into the crash barrier. It then toppled over the barrier due to the speed we were travelling at, tumbled around 3 times and the car landed and stopped on its roof. I have no recollection of this. I believe I was sleeping at the time.

My uncle and his family pulled up and ran down to the car.

Ultimately my dad died at the scene. His ribs were crushed by the steering wheel. My mum and I had serious life threatening injuries but luckily my little sister was unscathed.

We were all taken to the nearest hospital in Frankfurt. After being kept in a coma for 2 weeks due to my severe injuries I finally awoke. My right femur had been snapped in half. I had a long metal bar or brace running along my leg with 4 pin holes in my leg to hold the bone together. I had a skull fracture… fractured ribs… and a burn on my lower left leg.

Apparently 2 weeks earlier when the accident happened my uncle was informed that I only had a 25% chance of survival due to my injuries.

My mum died of severe brain injury a few days later.

So having now been allowed 2 weeks on to come out of coma… I looked towards the bottom of my bed and I could see my uncle and auntie sitting there. Obviously I knew straight away that something serious was wrong. They confirmed to me what happened. I remember asking if they were going to be my new mum and dad… I know that's strange but as you could imagine I was only 14 and in shock.

I started crying and so did they. Imagine lying in a hospital bed in a foreign country at 14 years old with a large metal bar sticking out of your leg and find out that both your parents had died… fuck me you wouldn't wish that on the devil let alone your worst enemy.

My uncle and auntie had to fly back to England. I stayed in that room for the next 3 days by myself before being flown to England.

My sister was only 6 years old when the accident happened. Although she has reasonable memory of our parents, it is obviously nothing like the memory I had as I was almost 15 at the time of the accident. It does pain me that my little sister cannot have experienced more time with our parents. She missed out on a lot. Unlike myself my sister should be very proud of the life she has led. She lived with my uncle and auntie until she was an adult and has been a bank manager for 20 years now. She has a good home and a son which she adores.

However she has had some other seriously bad times in her life also that at one point made her feel suicidal. I will explain more about this later.

My Deformed Leg

Due to the bone in my leg snapping in half it had to in itself be rebuilt. One end of the broken bone was fixed against the other end of the broken bone…but it was not set in a flush was so that new bone at the top end and bottom end could grow. This is what happened… my new bone grew quite a lot so I now have a femur in my right leg that is around twice as thick as normal.

The right femur is also about half an inch or so shorter than the left femur…you can clearly see that my right upper leg is bigger than my left upper leg.

This has caused a bit of a balance issue and in effect prevented me playing any contact sports like rugby or football.

My leg is a constant reminder of what happened to me and will remain so for the rest of my life.

Living with my Godparents and my first visit to Spurs since the accident

So when I first left chase farm hospital I went to live with my god parents in palmers green. I was close to them and my 2 God brothers Stel and Giggsy and God sister Rebecca growing up so I suppose it was a good place to be.

On the other hand and at first my sister lived with my Uncle (mums brother) who was at the scene of the accident.

Some weeks after the accident, the football season had started. That's when it hit me that I wasn't going to go to Spurs with my dad anymore. However I do recall quite a sad moment that happened around this time.

I have a vague memory of what happened next…. I believe I must have been in a manic episode of Bi Polar disorder, although I didn't know I had Bi Polar disorder at the time and it would be many years until I did so.

It was Saturday… I said to my god mother that I was going out. Ok so no real issues with that. At this time I was still on crutches with a huge brace over my upper right leg where I had my bone snapped in half in the car accident…. I told my good mother I was initially meeting with my mate at the park just a couple of hundred yards away.

However what was really happening in my mind is that I was somewhat hallucinating and hearing voices. Although Spurs weren't playing at home that day… the message that I was receiving or seeing in front of me was that the Spurs away game had been switched to a home game and that my dad would be waiting for me at the turnstile where would enter the ground.

So I powered off on my crutches. The ground is about 2 miles from my god parent's house. That's a long walk if you are on crutches. I remember sweating and often needed to stop. But I had to keep going as my dad would be waiting for me. I got to the other end of White Hart Lane…I was getting there but was knackered.

As I got closer I thought I must have been early as there was no one around. There certainly was not the amount of people that you would expect to see on match day. I got to where White Hart Lane meets Tottenham high road. I was fucked… I looked around and something didn't feel right. But I was just a few minutes away from reaching the meeting point with my dad.

I arrived at the turnstile and sat down at the entrance…and waited…still no one about…now my dad would have been coming from my right in the park lane direction….. I sat there for hours … I didn't know what time it was… I don't even know what time I got there…

I must have fallen asleep…it was a summer's day…I woke up when the darkness of the night sky was turning to light…. I had obviously spent the whole night there. My dad never turned up.

I think it is at that point in the morning I realised something strange had happened and that I must have been dreaming the whole thing.

However the fact of the matter is I was there at the ground sitting by the turnstile by myself on that Sunday morning.

I made my way back to my god parent's house… I was crying for most of the way back. There was clearly no game and my dad could not have come anyway as he was dead. This was a very traumatic period for me. My brain had clearly been damaged.

When I got back to my godparents early that morning my godmother had said that they were about to call the police 'Where have you been' she said. I just didn't know what to say. I just wanted to go and hide in a corner. I don't remember what I told her in the end but I didn't tell her about what had actually happened

Back to School after the accident

So it was about 5 weeks after the accident… the metal bar and pins had been removed from my leg and replaced with a large plastic brace…I still had my 2 crutches though. The school year was starting again. I suppose that those that be, thought I was fit enough to start school.

I arrived at school and met at the gate by a senior teacher. I didn't go to my classroom as I was taken to wait outside the assembly hall. Shortly after the assembly hall was packed.

Hundreds of seats were taken and other students standing on the sides.

Clearly there was some kind of reception for me… to let my fellow pupils know what had happened. I was called in. The hall was in total silence. I started to walk towards the front down the aisle that separated the chairs on the left from the chairs on the right. Most people turned round. 'They are looking at me' I thought. I got to the front and sat down facing everyone. The whole of the upper school were staring at me… the head teacher proceeded to let everyone know what had happened to me.

I don't know how I felt … I don't think I was embarrassed. Honestly the only thing I can remember whilst sitting there was that I was trying to calculate how many people were in the hall. I counted the row of chairs by the columns of chairs then the remaining people on the sides… I can't remember the number of people I had calculated but it was in the hundreds…I think I was trying to calculate that from all the people in the hall that day what were the chances that this had happened to me.

This was to be my last year at school and indeed we were the last year to study 'O Levels' which were' replaced by GCSEs the next year. I will tell you for sure now that O Levels are much harder than GCSEs. To get to college and study 'A Levels' back then you needed 3 'x O level' passes at grade A to C. I thing you need 5 GCSEs nowadays to be able to study 'A Levels thereafter. From the previous year I was on course to achieve 3 or 4 'O Levels' at grades A, B or C which would equate to 5 to 7 GCSEs at the same grade.

However as you can imagine my brain that year was frazzled. This was only 5 weeks after the car accident. Can you imagine what that was like for me? I had no desire or inclination to study or learn. My mind couldn't concentrate for long periods of time. I really didn't know why I went back to school so early. I needed therapy sessions not algebra lessons.

This continued the whole year. The exams I took were a waste of time. I failed them all.

However I retook GCSE exams the following year in a year course in 6th form. I achieved about 4 or 5 grades at A, B and C so that was fine.

Moving to my own house in Edmonton and starting my first job

I finished with school. I was 16 years old. I had lived with my godparents and then my uncle where my sister was living for about a year. It would have been 1987. With my share of the inheritance I purchased a 2 bedroom terraced house in Edmonton. This was about 3 miles from where most of my family and friends lived… might not seem a long way away but I couldn't just walk up the road like I used to and hook up with any mates.

At this same time I started working at a civil engineering company in the city as an office junior.

It was quite lonely coming home after work to an empty house. I couldn't meet up with my mates as at that time none of us had started driving and the 3 mile distance therefor was too far.

My grandparents lived in the high rise flats round the corner and my gran would always have a dinner ready for me at my house that my granddad would have dropped off earlier in the day.

However I remained lonely and although many of you might think that owning your house at 16 must have been great… it really wasn't.

I sort of wanted to go back and live with my uncle where my sister was and my 2 cousins…but that really wasn't an option.

Those first couple of years in that house were the worst times for me. This is when it really hit home what had happened. I felt so lonely and depressed. I wished for my family back. I had no one to fall back on or support me or comfort me. I often felt isolated and depressed.

ID Parade

I still use to meet up with my friends mostly at weekends. There was this one time that one of my mates Jorgin. We were having a walk around Enfield Town. We must have been around 16 years old. We were just looking around the shops, getting something to eat and minding our own business, when 2 undercover police officers approached us. They were looking for young lads to take part in an ID parade. They would give us £5 each… we agreed… but I was a little nervy… did they think that we were the possible culprits for a crime. Anyway, the feds got together around 10 lads of our age at the police station. The ID parade started… we couldn't see who was observing us but apparently it was an elderly woman. Anyway she bloody picked me! I don't know if the question she was given was who looks most like the offender or if she thought it actually was me…anyway the police let us go straight away as they weren't concerned that I was the offender.

When I got home I told my uncle what had happened. He accused me of committing the crime. He was a bit like that my uncle unfortunately.

Mathematics

Although in the end I found school life difficult due to the accident I soon discovered that I may have a minor gift for simple mathematics.

So as mentioned above my first job at the age of 16 was working in a Civil Engineering company. I was a junior at this company in London. Civil engineering is very much like being an architect for those of you that don't know what exactly Civil Engineering is.

My job was mainly to make drawings of sections of buildings demonstrating the various facets of a building. Obviously at that age although the drawings ended up looking quite complex they were reasonably easy to understand how to draw.

On one particular occasion there were a couple of guys off sick from work. There was a job that needed finishing and one of the major things left to do was to work out how many reinforcement metal bars would be needed for a particular building. Some bars are bigger than others in length and diameter and there was something else that needed calculating as part of the overall calculation.

"Let me have a go" I said to Andrew my manager at the time… he laughed… he probably thought that I was just messing around talking shit like I always was.

So this he what he done… he brought me over to one of the drawing boards and explained to me very quickly what needed to be done. He in his mind was just joking thinking I wouldn't know what the fuck he was talking about.

But I got it?! "Ok Andrew I've got it mate" and he laughed and walked off…

I started ploughing away at it… Andrew had disappeared to one of the other offices in our building… I'm guessing about half an hour later he returns… he sees me behind the drawing board. "What are you doing mate" he's said.

"I'm doing the calculation"… I said.

He walks over to me and has a look… he spends a couple of minutes reviewing what I had done … he looks at me…"How the fuck do you know how do that"… he said…

"It's easy" I said…

Well it turns out that the level of knowledge to do what I was doing was that of someone with maybe 10 years of experience and at least a degree in civil engineering! It simply wasn't realistic that I could have done what I done… not only that but I finished the calculation in 3 hours where it would usually take an actual professional with the knowledge a full day to make the calculation.

After I finished I was sent to see one of the bosses of the company…"Hello Spyros"… 'How are you son' he said…

"I'm good Simon"…I said

"Let me ask you" he said 'how did you manage to do that calculation'…

"I don't know"… I couldn't explain it…

"I just saw it in front of me and did it"

"Well I've got no idea… here's a fiver" he said 'go and get some lunch… take as long as you want'

… Now a fiver in those days was quite a bit of money… so that was a result..

There was another instance where I seem to excel with a mathematical/memory task. I'm guessing it was around 1999 and Ann, my girlfriend at the time and later to become my wife and I were living in our 2 bedroom flat in Southgate… I'm not sure if Sophia my first born had quite been born yet.

It was a Saturday Evening and we were watching a programme hosted by Cilla Black. I can't remember what the programme was called. Anyway within this programme a family would be chosen to perform a task. Actually it would be one member of the family that would be chosen and they would be given the task. They would then have one week to learn the task which they would then have to perform live on the following weeks show.

So the family were brought in and the task was at follows. The father of the family was giving a large card or sheet of paper with 100 single digits written out in a certain order… so for example 8024355457886466899843589 etc etc, until you reach 100 digits.

His task was to memorise those digits in that order. He had a week to learn the order and would then appear on the show that following week to see if he managed to do so.

As soon as he received the paper with the digits I turned to Ann and said "quick Ann quick let's get a sheet of paper"… I asked her to write out 100 digits in a line. That only took a couple of minutes.

So we were 15 minutes into the show so there was probably less than 45 minutes left before the programme would finish.

So Ann gave me the sheet with 100 digits and off I went. The first thing I had to work out was how to create a system that would make it easier for me to remember the numbers in order…I had never done anything like that before… you know memory games etc… Suddenly this came into my mind… I would separate the numbers into sets of 7 ie, the first 7 then the next 7 etc etc, in order. I would then dedicate a name to the first set and a name to the second set etc. the first set of 7 would be named after someone I knew whose name began with 'A' the second set would be named after someone that I knew whose name began with 'B' etc etc..

The reason I chose 7 digits per name is because that's how many digits were in a landline telephone number at the time. So I started. I would say a person's name beginning with 'A' and recite the first 7 numbers. I would repeat it a few times to make sure that I had memorised the first set of 7. I would then give the second set of 7 a name beginning with 'B' and would recite this set a few times until memorised and then revert back to the first set and recite those first 7 then followed by the second a couple of times. I would continue like this backwards and forwards. It took me about 40 minutes, this was still before the show had ended to memorise all 100 digits that Ann had written down in order. I read all 100 digits out to Ann in order. I don't know how I managed to do that task so quickly? The guy on the show had a week to do it. I did it in 40 minutes. Why don't you give it a go and see how you get on.

First signs of Bi Polar Disorder

So going back to when I was about 16 or 17 years old, my first unusual behaviour seemed to start.

I was around my grans flat probably for an extended visit. I don't know why but something happened in my mind that persuaded me to leave had my grans flat - completely naked! I got into the elevator and my thoughts were that I was going to have a look around the market downstairs.

I knew I was naked but for some reason my mind at the time was telling me that it was ok and normal. I got to the ground floor from the 19th floor in the elevator. I walked out. Luckily my granddad was walking back into the block so he saw me at the entry downstairs… he started shouting at me in Greek "what the fuck are you doing" and then dragged me back to the elevator and back to the flat. My gran was mortified… she couldn't understand and neither could I … I must have been in a manic episode but I had no idea what that was back then.

She called my uncle and he came round. It was assumed that I must have been Sleep walking but my uncle insisted I should see a doctor. I can't remember if I did or not. I do remember this though - this event happened around what would have been my mum's birthday. I was a little unwell in those few days around that time. Something like mild flu and was staying at my grans for a few days which was better than being by my-self in my small terraced house down the road. My grandparents it appeared were concerned for me that weekend and my grandmother was very weary of my movements.

I was 16 at the time and this was the time looking back that I also had the strongest beliefs I had the ability to fly. Now my grandparents lived on the 19th floor of her flats. There was a small balcony that you could go out onto which I often did. Whilst I was at my grans over these few days the feeling I could fly became stronger and stronger. My gran had her eyes on me as I kept going out to the balcony. Looking back now I have this feeling that I was going to try out this feeling and take a leap from her balcony. I don't know for sure if I would have done but the feeling I have is that there was a good possibility that I would have jumped. My gran starts having a go at me eventually after a few visits to the balcony and orders me back indoors and locks the balcony door.

Probably a year or so after these initial incidents, I had to attend (in my apparent but unknown at the time Bi Polar mind) an Alien meeting that was taking place in the Highlands in Scotland. I made my way to Kings cross on the Piccadilly line and then got on the train to Glasgow. After about 40 minutes the train arrived at Peterborough Station and the ticket guy was walking up and down the train checking people's tickets. I didn't have a ticket. I don't know why. Maybe I didn't think of it or thought it was not relevant as I was having a meeting with some superior aliens. I was being called to them to discuss a plan that they had to save the orphans of the earth. This was my destiny.

The ticket officer wanted me to get off the train as I didn't have a ticket nor it appears I could or even would pay. I told him that I couldn't and expressed the important reasons why I had to go to the highlands. Only he knows what must have been going through his mind when I said that! Anyway shortly afterwards 2 police officers got on the train and escorted me to the police station which was right next to Peterborough train station.

I appealed to them that I must get back on the train. They obviously either thought I was messing them around or I was crazy. They should in hindsight and with the knowledge I have of my illness now, sent me to hospital. Instead they put me back on a train to London.

So in these early years it appears my Bi Polar was coming out on top. Something was happening but I didn't know what. No doubt if my parents had been alive at the time this would have got sorted. My grandparents were too old to take charge of the situation and there was no one else really I wanted to get involved. I wanted it to pass whatever it was or just dismiss it.

One time I overheard my gran saying to her friend that I am mentally ill. This was around the time of the above events. I know from slight memory and later discussions I had been acting very strangely around this time… my gran was in the living room chatting with one of her fellow Greek Cypriot neighbours. In

Greek she said to the neighbour after explaining the earlier date when I went downstairs naked' he has mental problems' and that she thought that the accident had damaged my head' she was scared and didn't know what to do. I walked in on them with an angry face... looking at my gran... I think she realised that I had overheard what she had said. She tried to play the situation down. I wanted her to stop saying such things to people... why was she doing this? I would often get paranoid after that as to who else she had told such things to. On occasion due to this and when I was round my grans flat and she had visitors I found it difficult to show my face and would often hide away in the bedroom.

However the consequences of my Bi Polar disorder would get far, far worse over the forthcoming years which you will read about further within this book!

Tottenham Hotspur Memoirs

My dad first started going to spurs in 1966 with his brother who started going a few years earlier. Although they grew up in Archway which is Arsenal Territory, I think my uncle chose spurs due to the 1961 double winning team. My dad was hooked from that first game he went to which was Portsmouth at home in 1966. He met my mum in about 1968 and they got married in 1969. My mum started attending games with my dad.

It was May 1971 and Arsenal were' on course to win the double. That is the old English First Division which is now called the Premier League and the FA Cup. It was to come down to the last day of the season at White Hart Lane. If Arsenal won the game they would get the double.

I remember my mum telling me the story of when she was 6 months pregnant with me and that she had to queue up in her large impregnated state for 2 hours to get tickets for the game. It was early morning I believe and the queue was massive… going from Park Lane all the way towards Bruce Grove. To keep themselves occupied the queuing supporters would be singing their spurs songs…. Apparently it was quite loud… anyway this seems to have got me going… my mum said that in all the time she was pregnant with me that at that time when she was queuing for tickets was the time that I moved the most inside her belly… she said I must have been having a party in there…Unfortunately Arsenal went on to beat us and secure the double. For those Spurs supporters reading – the distress of supporting Spurs was there before I was even born LOL!

So I grew up loving football. I believe that any kid that goes to games from a young age will fall in love with football. Not just the football but the whole process of going to the game.

The whole experience was to become a massive part of my life.

It started off for me by going to watch Arsenal one week and Spurs the next week. It was around 1978 that I really started getting into football. For that first year I would go one week with my dad to Spurs and the next week to Arsenal with my granddad and 2 cousins who were all Arsenal supporters. In those days you could sneak in younger kids through the turnstiles. My granddad would pay a couple of pounds and ask for discounts for me and my younger cousin or just push us through without paying… how times have changed lol.

We always used to stand at the bottom of the east stand with the North bank to the right. However, I wasn't going there to support

Arsenal… it was a fun day out for me with my cousins. Yes I liked watching the football but I would never support Arsenal. I used to enjoy it when Arsenal lost or when their own supporters sung boring, boring Arsenal. I was always a spurs fan. It's in my blood you see.

My mum and dad were season tickets holders in the then east stand upper tier at Tottenham Hotspur. Due to work it was time for my mum to hand over her season ticket to me. However I remember the first game I was going to go to. I had an opportunity to go and visit my cousin that day and told my dad I wanted to go there and not the football. He said I couldn't and had to go with him to Spurs. Ok fair enough I thought. Let's see what this is all about. I was hooked.

I started going every home game with my dad after that. I would stay around my nans on Friday night after school. As you now know, she lived on the 19th floor in one of the flats above Edmonton Green Shopping centre.

I would be looking forward to going to bed on those Friday nights as I knew the next thing I would know would be when I woke up and it would be on the day of the game. When I did wake up it took a split second for my brain to function and determine whether we were at home or away that day. As soon as I self-confirmed we were at home I was buzzing. It really was the equivalent for me at that age as getting that buzz when you do a line of coke! Lol.

My dad would come round to my nans, we would eat breakfast and then onto the game. We always got in the ground at 2.40pm. 20 minutes before kick-off.

I haven't known for a very long time what it feels like to be happy. Certainly though when I look back to my childhood those Saturdays when Spurs were at home were fucking great.

The 1981 FA Cup final

In 1981 Spurs reached the FA Cup final. We were playing Manchester City. My dad had the 2 season tickets which entitled us to 2 tickets for the cup final. The problem was is that my Mum wanted to go to the Final. I pleaded with her to let me go. She offered me a pair of Roller Skates if I let her go. She also said that if there was a replay that I could go. I thought about it but couldn't take her offer. I had to go.

So I was staying around my grans on the eve of the cup final against Manchester City. Dad was to come and get me in the morning before we headed off to Wembley. I got up early that next morning. Super excited I was. I went downstairs for a walk around the market. Practically all of the market stalls were decked in blue and white scarves and flags. The market traders would be singing 'when the Spurs go Marching in' along with the shoppers that were already out that morning. It was buzzing and felt surreal. What a way to start the day off.

Off to Wembley we went. The atmosphere inside the stadium was electric. I had never heard anything like it. I was confident that we would win.

However, the game finished 1-1. There was going to be a replay. I was gutted! I lost out on a pair of Roller Skates and going to the replay which was arguably the greatest FA Cup Final of all time!

The 1982 FA Cup Final

We also got to the FA Cup final in 1982 against Queens Park Rangers. I didn't get to go to that cup final either although I can't remember the reasons why. We won in what was a crappy game which was the most important thing

The 1983 League Cup Final

In 1983 Spurs got to the League Cup Final. We were to play Liverpool. It doesn't get much bigger than that. It was a great atmosphere and fortunately this time around I got to be there. Spurs went one – nil up and the crowd went mad! With just 3 minutes to hold on, we were almost there. Liverpool Scored – Ronnie Whelan I believe. I was devastated. The game went to extra time. Liverpool had the momentum. They ended up scoring another 2 goals in extra time. We lost the final. This was a very painful experience for me. Still is slightly and this happened 40 years ago!

The 1984 UEFA Cup Final

In 1984 Spurs got to the UEFA cup final. This was to be played against Anderlecht from Belgium. The first leg took place in Anderlecht. The game finished 1 – 1. The second leg was played a White Hart Lane. This was the loudest I had ever heard the stadium. This was not only before that game, but also since. It was rocking inside the ground. Anderlecht went one nil up. There were faces of fear and panic everywhere. We had to win the cup. This was our 4th cup final in 4 years. The crowd were screaming with less than 10 minutes to go "Come on you Spurs….Come on you Spurs". I have never heard a noise like it. There was less than 10 minutes to go. The chanting continued it was non-stop then suddenly I heard a voice to my left of someone also shouting out "Come on you Spurs" that I had never heard before. It was my dad. Where we use to sit in the East stand upper tier there was never much singing but on that night it was the first time I recall my dad singing. I will never forget that moment. For some reason it has stuck with me. It made me feel happy and proud. I could see in the face of my dad what it meant to him. I turned back round, there were 7 minutes left. Spurs were on a constant frenzied attack mode. The crowd were trying to suck the ball into the net. The ball is in Anderlecht's penalty area. Graham Roberts gets the ball and bang it was in the back of the net. There was absolute pandemonium.

The game went to extra time and then penalties. This was my first experience of how terrifying a penalty shoot-out can be.

Spurs ended up winning 4-3 on penalties. It was a madness of celebrations. We lifted the cup and soon after we went home. I would love to have stayed around for the street party but I was too young and my dad had to get back.

That night was what football is all about. It stays with you forever. You just don't forget occasions like that. It was magic.

The 1987 FA CUP Final

In 1987 we reached the FA Cup Final again. We were playing Coventry City. We were heavy favourites. Going to the game we all felt at ease. Spurs were surely going to win. It had only been about 10 months since my parents died in the car accident. I had inherited the 2 Season tickets. I went to the game with my uncle, my dad's brother. As far as I was concerned it was going to be a great day out and finally get to see Spurs lift the cup at Wembley. With just a few minutes gone Spurs went One – nil up. However as the game went on City were getting better and better and they were playing out of their skins. On the other hand Spurs were playing like they were just expecting to win by just turning up.

We lost the final 3-2 and Coventry City deserved it. I couldn't believe it. I was gutted. How could we possibly lose with those players that we had at the time. You never get over losing a cup final especially if you are at the game.

Mark

By the time I was 16 I met 'Mark' at a bust stop on the way to Spurs. It was on Hertford Road in Edmonton. This was about 1.5 miles from the ground. We recognised each other at the bus stop. We had both been at the same house party the previous week. He and my mate Milti got into an argument. We laughed about it. So we soon discovered that we were going to the Spurs game. We became friends that day, and whenever Spurs would play at home we would go to the games together.

Along with a few others we started to go to away games also. Those were the days. There was nothing like a good away game, especially when Spurs won.

The 1991 FA Cup Semi Final
at Wembley – Tottenham v Arsenal

The history of Arsenal originally being from Woolwich in South London forms the main part of the rivalry between Tottenham and Arsenal….. "Fuck off back to South London" we sing to them… 'North London is ours'… a very brutal rivalry.

It was the 1991 FA Cup semi-final. This is when the FA Cup Semi Finals also began to be played at Wembley along with the final. It was Spurs v Arsenal. It was like a cup final. It almost felt like it didn't matter what happened in the final. This was the North London Cup final. Probably the biggest game between the 2 rivals ever. Arsenal were' the slight favourites.

I got tickets for me and my mate Wayne. We were travelling on a privately rented coach. It was a bit of a Hooligan coach to be honest. We got to the British Queen pub by White Hart Lane station about 7am in the morning. The pub was packed and jumping. It was a massive piss up and a sing along. By the time we got on the coach to go to Wembley we were wobbling from the alcohol consumed. It helped calm the nerves. This was one of the biggest games that either set of supporters would ever be going to. The pressure was intense. Imagine what it was like for the players. The atmosphere at Wembley stadium was crazy. It was kicking off between Spurs and Arsenal supporters everywhere.

When Paul Gascoigne scored his amazing goal the crowd went mental. However, Arsenal pulled a goal back just before half time to make the half time score 2-1 to Spurs.

This really increased the pressure that we were feeling on the terraces. People spent the second half holding their hands over their head and biting their finger nails. We expected the worse but then….Gary Lineker got put through….he just had the keeper to beat…he kicks the ball. Oh my God he's scored – 3-1 to Spurs – absolute pandemonium. These were the craziest scenes I had ever seen in my whole life at a football stadium. Supporters were literally flying around everywhere.

The ecstasy that you feel on such an occasion cannot be explained. For those 10 or 15 seconds after that third goal went in was like nothing you can ever experience.

We won the game and everyone headed back to their part of North London with thousands of us returning to Tottenham for celebrations. What a fucking night.

It was a couple of weeks later and a typical evening down our local pub… the Cherry Tree in Southgate North London. It was only a couple of weeks before the 1991 FA Cup final. Spurs were to play Nottingham Forest. I couldn't get a ticket through my membership so thought I wasn't going to go.

My mate Kevin enters into the pub… "Spyros" he said.. "I've been offered 2 tickets for the cup final"… great news… however the guy that was selling them wanted £80 each for them… that was practically a week's wages back then.

Kevin and I pondered over it for a while over a game of pool and a beer…we both decided that we really couldn't afford it so didn't go… we ended up winning the cup… in fact that was the last time spurs won the FA cup… no need to say how gutted we were that we didn't go! I ended up watching the game with my mate Wayne at home. We went crazy when Spurs scored. After the game we jumped into the car and headed off to White Hart Lane for the celebrations. It was a great night celebrating with the tens of thousands of other Spurs supporters.

1992 Feyenoord Away – UEFA Cup

Feyenoord away…. Fuck me what a 24 hours that was. So there was a good few thousand spurs that travelled away to Holland for a Cup Winners Cup tie. Going on the boat crossing the English Channel was madness, a drunken frenzy of singing and chanting.

We arrived at the port in Holland and then we got back on the coach. As we approached the stadium there was a lot of traffic. A local female journalist was in a car next to us. She was filming us in the coach having a jump around and a sing along… she was trying to entice us to act in a rowdy way… stupid …. "Oh look the English are here let's provoke them to act in the stereotypical way" lol!!

We got to the stadium quite early but the home stands were almost full already… they were rocking…the ground was bouncing! There was a lot of provocation from the home fans next to us. We were separated by a massive fence… but the fence was week. Both sets of fans were trying to break through the fence to get at each other…somehow at the bottom of the fence where it met the pitch level, slightly collapsed and it kicked off there. There were massive surges from both sets of fans but the police quickly had it under control.

We were situated in the lower end of this particular stand with Dutch fans directly above us who could comfortably look down and over us. One Dutch guy starts pissing from the upper stand down onto us…then missiles and coins were thrown back at him.

There were flares going off all over the place and fireworks but what happened next was incredible.

A rocket/firework was set off at the complete opposite end of the ground towards us. We saw it coming, it looked massive… 'Fuck me' it was coming towards us. Here it comes then smash… it crashed straight into the advertising boards at the base of the upper tier. This rocket must have been about 2ft long and had a circumference of a street lamp pole. If it had landed about 3 feet higher and hit someone it would have gone straight through them. They would have died for sure!

We lost the game and were then kept back in the ground for an hour to stop us mingling with the notorious Feyenoord supporters. Spurs and Feyenoord have history when it comes to violence. When Spurs played there back in 1974, it made front page headlines due to the amount of trouble. There was thousands on both sides rioting and there were some stabbings. It was carnage. This was when the so called English disease of Hooliganism began abroad.

Anyway, we made it back home safely. Although we lost it will be 24 hours I can never forget.

1999 Legaue Cup Final

It was 1999 before our next cup final. This was the league cup final to be played at Wembley against Leicester City. I was with Mario and Mark from what I can remember. The atmosphere was great but the game was really poor. Then just with a couple of minutes to go we got the winning goal. I was buzzing with happiness and also relief that I had finally got to see Spurs lift a cup at Wembley.

2002 League Cup Final

A few years later we were in the League Cup final again. We were playing Blackburn Rovers. However this time we were playing at the Millennium Stadium in Cardiff. Wembley stadium was being rebuilt so major games were transferred to the Millennium stadium for a period of time.

Once again Spurs were clear favourites for this game. We got to a massive Spurs allocated pub in Cardiff before the game. Everyone was off their heads on alcohol and cocaine. A large group of local boys – Cardiff supporters turned up outside. There is a bit of rivalry between Cardiff and teams like West Ham, Chelsea, Millwall and Spurs. It is a sort of an England v Wales thing. Spurs supporters started steaming out of the pub. There was a proper kick off between the 2 sets of fans. However it didn't last long as there were so many Police about.

The atmosphere at the Millennium stadium is fantastic. Spurs supporters were confident of winning the cup. However it didn't end up like that. Spurs lost 2-1.

We went back to the pub after the game. There were hundreds of Spurs supporters in there drowning their sorrows in pints of lager. Many supporters were staying overnight in the Cardiff area. I think that Mario, Tim and I were supposed to be driving back to London that night. It turned out that Tim and I decided to stay over in Cardiff and Mario drove himself back home. So we were in the pub having a drink amongst the hundreds of other Spurs supporters, when 2 Welsh girls walked into the pub. Probably their local pub but what were they doing coming into a pub full of rowdy Spurs supporters. The girls were given a bit of banter and flak but it was all in good humour and they also found the funny side of it to be fair. I said to Tim 'let's go over and chat to them' and so we did. We got in there first lol…I am sure there were many other Spurs boys eyeing them up. We ended up spending a few hours with them. Tim and I found a hotel in Bristol…….

2008 League Cup Final – Spurs V Chelsea

Most people believe that the biggest football rivalry in London is Tottenham V Arsenal. This is true but I can tell you for sure that Tottenham v Chelsea is not very far behind.

Over recent years Chelsea have become almost as big a rival as Arsenal. The reasons go back to the rivalry around the 1967 FA Cup final with all sorts of shenanigans going on, which intensified once again with some big games around the time when Pochettino was our manager in mid to late 2010s.

However what many people don't realise is the shear hatred between the 2 sets of supporters. This comes from anti sematic chants by Chelsea supporters against spurs supporters who have a large Jewish following. This hatred for as long as I remember has spilled out to hooliganism between the 2 sets of fans which over the years when looking at 2 particular sets of fans consistently fighting each other in the whole of England it would be when Spurs play Chelsea.

2008 was a big occasion when Spurs met Chelsea in the League Cup final at Wembley.

Chelsea we're slight favourites. Our private coach was organised which met us about 8am at a pub in Edmonton many hours before the game was scheduled to kick off. The usual partying etc started that morning. It was time to get on the North Circular Road again and make our way back to Wembley which is about half an hour's drive away. On approach to Wembley with maybe a mile or so to travel, a Chelsea coach pulled up next to us in the other lane. The banter and songs started. They were shouting out at us from their coach and we were doing the same. We were approaching the area where the coaches would be parking. The Chelsea coach suddenly went very quiet. They must have realised that we were going to park in the same place. The coaches ended up parking pretty much next to each other. The Chelsea supporters must have realised that we were now going to face up to each other out on the street outside the coaches. They shit themselves.

The Spurs supporters got off the bus but the Chelsea coach driver wouldn't open the doors to let the Chelsea supporters out. We started banging their coach and rocking it side to side and then after a while we left.

We were a coach of hooligans or guys who were up for a fight if it presented itself whereas in all fairness the Chelsea coach did not contain the like-minded people. They were Chelsea fans but not the hard core that you might associate with Chelsea's ultras. We realised this and were just fucking with them. There was no intention to physically attack them as we knew it wasn't any of their firm. Had it been a section of Chelsea's firm then it would have kicked off big time between the 2 sets of fans. There would have been proper blood-shed between the 2 rival sets of fans.

The rule is if there is such a thing when it comes to football violence is that you only fight with like-minded people. Firms do not attack rival supporters in general unless they are game or part of an opposing firm.

Anyway, we got into the ground and the atmosphere was buzzing – mainly made so by Spurs supporters amazing noise. Chelsea were favourites to win but Spurs were really playing well from the off.

We got to extra time and Spurs scored the winner. There were absolute mad scenes. When we lifted the cup having beat Chelsea in the final it was one of the happiest moments in my Spurs life. What a fucking day.

My Last games at the old White Hart Lane Stadium

2014

I lived in Spain from 2004 until 2011 so got to see very few games over those years. Only on my short breaks back to England could I attend the games. However I watched all of the games at Linekers bar in Marbella. Whether Spurs were playing home or away the game was being screened live – so actually never missed a game.

I moved back to England in 2011 and attended games when I could. My drinking problem was very bad at this stage. One of the last games that I attended at the old White Hart Lane stadium was against West Ham. This is what happened.

So there was only about thirty minutes left before kick-off. Big game West Ham - especially for them- Tottenham away -that's their cup final! Lol. Anyway I came out of the Bricklayers Arms pub and turned right on the High Road and just metres where White Hart Lane meets the high road. You could see that West Ham supporters were being held back by a line of police. There were about 300 of their firm at the top of white hart line. For those that don't know, when most of the larger clubs from London travel to another London club on match day, there will often be a group of around 300 of the away fans that travel together on the underground mainly as part of a tribal entrance to the away territory trying to show that they are fearless and have come to step over your area and make noise and threats at the same time.

Anyway I was now at the corner of White Hart Lane and the High Road. I could see the police line in front of the West Ham fans and about another 10 police on horses in front of them. I was drunk so couldn't make sensible judgements lol..West Ham we're chanting their usual Anti Tottenham songs. I crossed the road directly in front of them. As I did I looked over at the West Ham fans and spat in their direction but on the floor. Everyone on the front line of their fans saw me do that, then …. Shit!..The whole of their crowd started surging forward. The police were struggling to hold them back…. Fuck my life flashed before me if they got through I would have been battered… a policeman on horseback quickly shuffled me across the road… fuck that was close…what a stupid thing to do but I was off my head as usual.

One line should do it!!'
It fucking turned me into a zombie for 2 hours.

Spurs were playing at home. It must have been 2014. I went to Rudolph's pub that was in front of the stadium. It was always packed in there on match days. It no longer exists now due to the new stadium.

I was to meet Mario and Mark there before going to the game. I got there early and ordered my first drink. I went to the toilet. A couple of boys were having a sniff of what I thought was cocaine. "Leave me a line please mate" I said to one of the lads.

"There you go mate" one of the guys left me a good sized line by the basin. One big snort.... Aaaahhh that should do the trick I thought!

Obviously I thought I had just snorted a line of Cocaine. It turns out it was fucking ketamine …that's horse bloody tranquilliser. I walked to the beer garden. My head started spinning. I sat on a stool by the bar and then bang, I turned into a paralysed zombie! I sat there with my eyes closed and semi asleep for 3 hours. I could hear what was going on around me.

People were asking are you ok mate? I managed to mumble the word ketamine out. They knew what had happened. The bar staff got wind but as they knew me the decided it was best to just leave me sitting there until I recovered. It took me 3 fucking hours. Almost motionless for the whole time but I was still relatively aware of what was going on around me. I could hear some of the boys winding me up that brought a small smile to me in my intoxicated closed eyed state. Thankfully I got through it. However I missed the game. I saw Mark and Mario after the game. I told them what had happened and they pissed themselves laughing.

They will never let me down for what happened. What a fuck up of a day!

Taking into account the ketamine episode and fronting the ICF on Tottenham High Road I knew then that I was starting to endanger myself by just going to Spurs. Something had to change.

I was not able to attend another Spurs game until 2022 at the new Tottenham Stadium. You will find out later why!

Smoking Weed

I started smoking week in my late teens… we all did back then… absolutely loved it. Mates would often come round to mine as I had my own place and they at our age were still living with their parents. We use to piss ourselves laughing when smoking the weed and then of course get the munchies. Back then we use to literally crawl on the floor bursting with laughter. The weed as many of you will know makes you come out with a lot of delusional shit. I was the main instigator of comical crack ups. People use to beg me to stop as they were laughing so hard it would give them pain in their ribs. Funny days…

I kept smoking weed until I was about 23 years old but then suddenly when I smoked it I would get this tight feeling in the heart area. It was like one of my arteries was being squeezed so the blood couldn't pass through. The weed was clearly affecting my heart somehow. I had multiple investigations at the time to try and found out what exactly was causing that pain but they couldn't detect anything back then.

It wasn't until around 2007 when I lived in Spain that I discovered the probable cause of the pain. In a general check up at the private hospital I attended, they detected a fault on one of my aortic valves.

Basically where you have the base of one of the valves there should be three triangular flaps that push blood out. However I was born with just 2. So the process of pushing blood out would in effect act a little slower. Now when you smoke weed it slows down your blood circulation unlike cocaine which speeds it up. So when smoking the weed the blood flow going through that valve would be too slow and in effect it would cause a slight blockage at the base and the blood would move through too slow. This would create the feeling of blockage and tightening which caused the pain.

I stopped smoking weed when I was 23.

Cyprus 1990

So now I am going back to before my Tottenham memoirs. It was time for my first holiday abroad with one of the lads. On this holiday in Cyprus, Jorgin and I would have been 18 or 19 years old.

I can remember being at the departure lounge at Luton Airport. I started playing Bee Gees music on the stereo I was taking with me. I played it louder and louder and started dancing. It was crazy. The whole departure lounge then stood up and started dancing also. This was a great way to begin the holiday.

The holiday was in the area of Ayia Napa. This was becoming the new Ibiza for young holiday makers. The clubs were full and the atmosphere was great. We would go to the beach in the day and then clubbing at night.

Also during the day we took part in 5 a side football. There were 4 teams that were created literally by guys that were on the same flight as us on the way out. We had the same teams every day. This was around the time when arguably for that short period Paul Gascoigne was the best player in the world. I loved Gascoigne. He was possibly my favourite Spurs player of all time. There were a couple of moves/or tricks that I learned from watching him at that time. During these 5 a side games I would try out the tricks and they worked. Considering I had a fucked up leg due to the accident,

I done pretty well. I was voted player of the holiday tournament. This was a very proud moment for me and something I will never forget. I cannot play football on a full sized pitch as this generally means 'full contact football' rather than 5 a side football which is more about control and passing. Full contact football would mean tackles and that would have been too dangerous for my leg.

One day Jorgin and I decided we needed a buzz… at that age we has started regularly smoking weed. We didn't know where to get any from and weren't sure who to ask. So one night before a night out we were having a drink in the apartment and one of us came up with the smart idea of snorting some strong Greek coffee powder lol!… that might work!

We rolled up a note each and put a line of coffee each on the table. We were to do it at the same time… 1,2,3….. and sniff!!… Jorgin started sneezing … my eyes watered…did we get a buzz… did we fuck… what a disaster that was.

It was a good holiday and gave me the taste of maybe wanting to live in a warmer country. It was also our first experience of being surrounded by girls 24 hours a day. Over the next few years there would be a few more 'mates' holidays but this first one in 1990 was the best

House Music all night long

I'm not sure what year it was but it was around the late 1980's to the early 1990s. This is when the Ministry of Sound nightclub opened at the Elephant and Castle. House music was becoming popular and this club was one of the ones to go to for that kind of music.

There were a few different rooms playing different kinds of music. There was House, New York Garage etc.

Welcome to the world of Ecstasy. Well I mean the drug form. The clubs were packed with clubbers that were off their tits on drugs. They were dancing for hours on end. It was mental. It was like tribal cult that danced to the sounds like they were chants from a futuristic land.

You could see that some were dancing and having delusions at the same time. I danced with euphoric thoughts of delusions of grandeur. This would be become quite common for me over the forthcoming years although I had stopped actually taking ecstasy pills within a year from that first time. However something was continuing to cause the euphoric delusions thereafter?....

So by now Mark and I were quite euphoric on the buzz that we were getting from the ecstasy pills. We were dancing away with everyone else like we were in some kind of dance ritual. I clocked a small group of lads standing not too far away from us. They were staring in the direction of Mark and I looked at Mark when I realised who they were. 'Mark… See those 3 over there… their West Ham I said… proper ICF (Inter City Firm) that's the name of West Ham's hooligan firm. Mark looked at them and recognised a couple of their faces also. There had been an incident at a Tottenham v West Ham game a few weeks earlier when it kicked off outside The Bricklayers Arms. Mark and I happened to be in the pub that day and were part of a group of Spurs that ran out to 'Front' the West Ham Boys. We recognised these lads as being part of the West Ham firm that day.

They were looking at us. Fuck me I've come out to have a dance and pull a bit of skirt not to have a fucking row.

They headed towards us.

"Alright boys you good" they said. They were off their tits from the pills.

We smiled back at them in anticipation of what was going to happen next.

"Good scrap the other week" one of them says.

"Oh yeah yeah… right" we said. We all shock hands and had a fucking cuddle. It was fucking ridiculous. That never bloody happens.

Tottenham and West Ham having a fucking cuddle. It was strange but funny. Can you imagine us two 'Yids' (spurs supporters) and 3 proper West Ham who would under different circumstances be prepared to punch each-others lights out… having a cuddle in a fucking nightclub… hilarious… the wonders of ecstasy.

So the night had ended… it was probably about 7 in the morning and we got in Marks car to drive home…we were fucked and to be honest Mark should not have been driving mainly due to tiredness let alone the ecstasy intake. It wasn't long whilst driving back I turned to my right and Mark was fucking sleeping… I don't know how long his eyes had been shut for… I shouted and shoved…"wake up" I said… I kept my eye on him the whole way back… if I hadn't been watching him then anything could have happened as I know so well. Sleeping in a car now has literally become impossible for me since my dad fell asleep at the wheel in the accident.

Los Angeles 1991

In 1991 I left my job at the Civil Engineering Company. Although I enjoyed the work, ultimately I knew that this wasn't going to be my future. I struggled concentrating for more than a couple of hours at a time. My brain would get frazzled. I would get bored too easily.

This was not to be my life.

Around this time my mate Aydin and I decided that we would go on a long holiday to Los Angeles and find out what fortunes that would bring for us.

So after months of planning me and my mate Aydin arrived in Los Angeles. We didn't know how long we would be there for… we had an open mind… let's see what happened. I was still 19 at the time and Aydin would have been 20. The drive from the airport was a good 45 minutes to our destination which was Hollywood Boulevard. We had agreed a long term rent for an apartment in Hollywood Boulevard so we're looking forward to that. I remember thinking in the taxi on the way there how spaced out everything seem to be. I don't know why but I just had this feeling that LA wasn't going to be what we thought it might. Growing up you were' always aware of LA due to films and celebrities and money and parties. This is what we were expecting.

Anyway, we lived in a 2 floor apartment. Well the upper floor was a large Mezzanine. Aydin took the upstairs and I took the downstairs.

Soon after being in LA we met up with another English guy that was a couple of years older than us. His name was Robert. He had been living in LA for a while and was trying to make it as an actor. Anyway one weekend he said he was working security at a 'rave' in Compton which is one of the tougher 'hoods' in LA. He invited us to come over and we agreed… of course, why not? Now this part I found strange.

He said that as a security guard he would be carrying a gun for the event… 'No way' we thought…how did that come around… he wasn't an American so I don't see how he could be licenced.. if he was telling the truth it must have been illegal… anyway we weren't sure as to whether to believe him… anyway we went to the rave and it was good fun… no problems but it turned out Rob was packing a gun… what the fuck!! Made us a little nervous about the place we were at but ultimately it turned out fine.

Straight Out of Compton to Watts

So it must have been sound 5am and 7am in the morning when the rave in Compton had finished. Rob, Aydin and I were driving home after the evening's festivities. We decided to stop off at a 7/11… sunlight was beginning to shine…we were tired and fucking starving… we were in Watts.

We went into the 7/11 and from what I remember purchased about 3 burritos each… we came back outside and started scoffing our faces. Just In front of us there was a group of 6 or 7 young guys approaching us…. "What you guys doing around here" … one of them said… which was said in a tone that left me quite nervy… we were strangers in their 'ends' and they wanted to know why!

Rob took control of the situation …he explained that we were returning from a Rave in Compton… they guys were a little suspicious of us… I don't know if they thought we were undercover cops or something. I got the impression that white guys that aren't from Watts generally don't stop by there… so I could see their suspicion… anyway it settled down and then actually became funny… the conversation began as to who was the better music artist 'Prince or Michael Jackson' …. Most of them thought Prince… but us 3 white guys all thought Michael Jackson.

There was a good bit of humoured banter that went on between us for five or ten minutes… it was good fun and a laugh…then a few fist pumps exchanged before we left… ultimately we were glad we met these lads and I think they were glad they met us… will never forget that morning… a group of lads as we all were standing outside a 7/11 in Watts at 5 am in the morning discussing who was the better Artist Prince or Michael Jackson… just a classic…

Watts looking like a prison - unfortunately one of the lasting memories that I have of Watts is that many if not all the homes had metal bars covering the windows of homes. What a shame these lads that I had just met had to live like that. It is not their fault it is the fault of the government and wider society that has allowed Watts to become such a place of danger that the locals need keep themselves banged up in their own homes to protect themselves… it comes down to the subject of poverty again. The concept of poverty has evil underpinnings in that allow a person to be poor is firstly evil in itself and thereafter the actions of many in poverty can become evil. Poverty is the pre-set of crime.

If they are literally fighting for their lives day after day to make ends meet, to put food on the table to look after their children then a human being may be forced to act out wrongly to survive.

However this cannot for the main be their fault. It is the fault of their brothers and sisters being all other American citizens and governing bodies who have allowed this circle of evil to exist. There is no reason why around the world and especially in America why there should be any poverty. There is plenty of money to go around. They say money is the root of all evil and that is right. But the evil starts from those who have so much wealth but do nothing or very little to help others. God gave these people Free Will to do more and better for their less fortunate beings but as stated in most instances they do not. The list for more and more money that is then not used correctly is work if the devil. I will talk about this more later on.

Earthquake

It was about 7am. Aydin was sleeping upstairs in the mezzanine. I was down stairs. All of a sudden the fucking building starts shaking and the floor is moving… we both woke up immediately. Aydin looked down over from the Mezzanine to where I was on the floor below… I stood up and looked at him… the whole building was really moving and the floor felt like we were riding a wave… "It's a fucking earthquake" I shouted. We were excited couldn't believe it … coming from England we had never experienced an earthquake before…. It must have gone on for about 10 seconds or more…at the age we were it seemed exciting but no doubt for many others it would have been very scary and costly.

Superman

One of our neighbours was a Guy called Emmett North Junior… a musician trying to make his way in the pop world. He was actually very successful and had been in some very famous bands and singers. We got to know him quite well and he was a good guy He at a guess would have been around 40 at that time. One of his mates was the actor from Superman …. You know the 3 evil guys that came to earth and challenged Superman –One of General Zod's guys - well the big scary looking guy was one of Emmett's mates so we met him on a few occasions.

USA V UK

One time Emmett and a few of his mates met with us at our apartment. We decided to have a beer drinking game - USA v England lol! There were 3 yanks and 3 of us English.

Now you yanks need to realise that it is part of British culture to drink excessively. Not only that, many of us start drinking alcohol as young as 13 on a regular basis. Not saying it's a good thing but that's just the way it is over here.

Anyway at least 3 guys ended puking up…. The English team smashed them… we were cultured drinkers… so that's just a warning to the Americans - don't have a drinking competition with a Brit lol!

So, our days would consist of getting up and then off out to discover LA… you know the usual places.

Back home in the afternoon and get ready for a quiz show that we watched every day, usually with a couple slices of pizza. Every day there would be a challenge me v Aydin as to who would get the most answers on the quiz show… most days it got heated between us and we kicked of loads of times. I think a fucking knife got pulled out once when we overly pissed each other off.

Cher

One night we were queuing up to get into a nightclub on Hollywood Boulevard… using our trusted fake ID cards! We got to the front of the queue and all of a sudden the singer Cher turns up and is standing right next to me…she went in and soon after we followed in… I tried to find her… don't know why but anyway she was nowhere to be seen. They probably had some private room where VIPs go… I was gutted ….

"Why are you so gutted" Aydin said…

"I wanted to meet her and you know she might have been up for something"! Lol…

Aydin pissed himself laughing. "What the fuck would Cher want to do with you".. he laughed. Well that was delusional me lol!

Hanging out with a Rock Star

However, the most famous 'Rock star' we met who actually wasn't a Rock Star at all was a Swedish guy called Thomas. He was actually homeless… a vagrant… we bumped into him a couple of times outside 7/11 on Sunset Boulevard. He always wore his tight blue jeans and matching jean jacket. He had long fuzzy blonde hair. He actually did look like a Rock Star.

He came and stayed with us for a few days.

One time we went to the big shopping centre in Beverly Hills. We would enter the expensive boutique clothes shops. Aydin and I would act as if we were Thomas's entourage and we would pretend that Thomas was a Rock star… he really did look like one!… we would go around the shop and look at clothes that cost hundreds if not thousands of pounds… the shop assistants would eagerly assist us…. But of course we bought nothing as we had Fuck all money lol… it was a very funny time.

San Francisco

I suppose half way through our 3 month stay in LA we wanted to explore other areas. We purchased a crappy second hand car for about $500. We decided to take the coastal route up to San Francisco. It took a couple of days and one night we stayed in Santa Barbara. For some reason we decided on a theme tune for our journey that we ended up singing all the way to Frisco and all the way back.

"Are you going to Scarborough Fare,

Parsley, Sage, Rosemary and Thyme

Remember her, the one who lived there

She was once a true love of mine"

I don't know why we chose that song thought?! lol

Anyway we arrived in Frisco but didn't know where to head for accommodation etc. So as we approached the city we stopped off as there were a couple of guys walking passed. We asked them. "Hello mate" I said… we are new in town. We just wanted some advice on where to stay etc.

As soon as one of the guys spoke we realised he must have been gay as he acted and spoke in a very camp way… so did his mate.

He gave us some directions then said to us. "Hey do you guy's workout" …. 'We love your accent' they said… they were hitting on us lol… well we were in San Francisco… we thanked them … and we hurried along…

Seeing the Golden Gate Bridge, Alcatraz and driving up and down the incredibly steep roads was all good.

We checked into a cheap hotel. Went out that night… but from what I can remember our fake IDs weren't working as well as they were in LA… can't remember where we ended up.

We only stayed in San Francisco for a day or two… we wanted to keep driving and just see where we ended up… could be Canada… but our money was low and my credit card bills were piling up. We had to go back to LA…. Singing, 'Are you going to Scarborough fare' all the way back of course!

Overall the stay in LA was 'ok'. Ultimately we didn't have enough money to do everything we wanted. I suppose it was cool meeting some famous people like Cher, a band member of the Smiths and Alice in Chains before they became famous. There were some fun times but when we departed I was left feeling a little disappointed about the experience. There was something missing from our time there. I think we may have expected a little too much out of LA.

Grecian Cypriana 1991

So we returned from LA. I needed a job. I was properly skint. All credit cards had been maxed out. I heard through a friend that there were job vacancies at a major travel tour operator in Crouch End – North London. There was a vacancy in the accounts department. I met with Len the manager of the department. All went well especially as he was also a season ticket holder at Spurs. I got the job. It was Ok but very soon I started having the same feelings of boredom and my brain becoming frazzled after a couple of hours. I would get tired and demotivated quite easily.

One time I fell asleep on a shelf in the large store cupboard. They had to send a search party out for me. The boss was pissed off. I really started to wonder why my brain could only work for a certain amount of time before turning off. Was it damaged during the car accident I thought?

I stayed at the job for about 2.5 years but I was longing for something else. I needed an escape. I felt my life to be quite dull, lonely and unfulfilling.

My friend Milti came and worked there for a while. In the Spring of 1994, Milti decided he wanted to become a holiday rep for the company. He was to head over to the Greek Island of Corfu in May 1994. Soon after another of my friends Wayne and I decided to join him. So i left Grecian Cypriana's head office to become one of their reps in Corfu.

Holiday Rep Corfu 1994

Although I have never really been happy in my adult life there was a period of 5 months when I worked as a Holiday rep on the Greek Island of Corfu that was amazing fun. This was in 1994 when I was 22 almost 23 years old… 2 of my mates from England, Wayne and Milti were with me over there working as reps also.

The main duties of holiday reps were to pick up the companies' holiday makers from the airport and then take them to their hotels in the various destinations around the island.

You would see to the customer needs or concerns throughout their stay etc.

The other important duty of a holiday rep was to persuade the customers to book onto as many excursions as you could… this could be a boat trip to a small neighbouring island for a beach BBQ… or a Greek Dinner and dance night out or entertainment by the reps on a night out.

The reps night out would include us acting out our own version of Cilla Black's 'Blind Date' or being the 'Take That' pop band and doing choreographed dances to their music.

They were great times… we all went out parting every night without fail… basically we got pissed every night for 5 months had 3 hours sleep a night and then get up and went to work, then at night do the same again… it was fucking knackering especially when you consider that we were chasing women every night and most of the time with success… if you know what I mean. After all that, having just 3 hours sleep a night was getting to me… I would often sleep on the boat on excursion or on the bus or wherever I could during the day providing I had time…. Just to keep me going… looking back I don't know how the fuck I did it. There was one occasion where I was so knackered that ended up being funny but a little embarrassing.

A rep from another tour operator had spotted me at the airport…. We spoke on a couple of occasions when we bumped into each other. Anyway she made it clear that she liked me and I liked her. She worked in the North of the Island and I was based towards the South so we didn't really live that close to one another. Anyway arrangements would be made for me to go up and see her in a few days' time. I was excited… we sent messages to each other through other reps on route passing through our individual resorts and villages etc…remember there were no mobile phones back then. It was quite funny I think half the reps on the island must have known about us… so there was a lot of excitement and anticipation about our meet up.

So the day arrived… I headed up towards where she was staying… got there … all great, but I was seriously tired. We decided straight away to get down to business…. I got on top of her… collapsed and fell asleep…woke up the next morning …. She had already fucked off to work… leaving just a note "thanks for a great evening"… I felt so embarrassed… I got out of the resort sharpish… It wasn't too long before the word got around to the other reps that had been part of the process for our meet. I was fucking rinsed for days… so embarrassing but a little funny at the same time.

The party animal was now set in me. However the holiday season was over. As I said it was probably the best 5 months of my life. I thought about doing it again the next year but it never happened.

Timeshare 1995

So I was about to sell timeshare… I know it had a bad name but that was from people out on the Costa del Sol etc enticing people from the beach to go to a presentation and be awarded various gifts in doing so. They were told 'all you have to do Mr and Mrs Smith is sit there for 1.5 hours then if you are not interested then just tell the sales advisor at the end and you will get your free gifts'. Little did the customers know that they were going into a high pressured environment where often they agreed to a deal that they would regret at a later time'.

However, having said that Timeshare can work well for people if you buy weeks in the right resort that has high power within the exchange system. We were selling timeshares within an exchange system called RCI – Resort Condominiums International. It all looked pretty good to me.

So, anyway the sales room was in Borehamwood in North London. It was practically next to Elstree studios where they film 'Eastenders'. I went there for a 1 day training session. All straight forward stuff I suppose. Basically, the timeshares that were on offer were linked to a company called RCI as mentioned above. This was a large pool of hundreds of timeshares spread around the world where you could exchange your 1 or 2 week's Timeshare, let's say in Spain to stay at a timeshare anywhere else in the world. We watched videos and were given brochures and trained how to sell the timeshare.

So I went back to the office the next day. This was my first day of work selling timeshare. There were 30 other sales people there waiting to greet the customers who we called 'UPS'.

As the new kid on the block you were at the back of the line to meet the Ups. The best sales people were at the front of the line… I'm sure you get it.

There was an element of arrogance amongst the better sales people. They used to think they were the dog's bollocks – however they hadn't met me yet!

There were plenty of Unqualified Prospects (UPS) coming in that day so I was sure to get my chance. So I did. I was called through to meet my first potential customers. I picked them up from the waiting room and took them to the sales room. They sat down and I sat down opposite them.

When you are trained you are instructed to make friends as such with the potential clients. This would involve between 1 to 1.5 hours of chit chat. This was I suppose, to create a trust between us two parties and find some common ground etc. The UPS knew that they were coming in to be sold timeshare and 99% of them had no intention of doing so as they were only interested in the FREE gift that they would receive for taking part in the presentation.

They sat there, arms crossed looking at me. I could see they seemed a little nervous and protective in anticipation as to what was going to happen.

I looked round to the rest of the Sales room. The sales reps were having their chit chats with the UPS.

I said "hello" to my couple. We started chatting. I started asking this couple who are at least double my age, questions about their lives and on things that I really wasn't interested in. It all felt a bit fake and disingenuous.

Only about 5 minutes had passed and I thought "Fuck this" I can't keep small talking for another hour. So I decided to change my plan of action.

I took a sheet of paper and on it I wrote in very large writing

'£5,000'. I turned the sheet round and I would show the couple the figure. I then asked them "do you know why have written this number down and showed you"

"No" they said.

I replied "This is the amount of money that you will be spending with me today". I then smiled at them and they would laugh. It was an ice breaker. It made them feel less nervy and they knew exactly what my intentions were that day. They were now at ease and we would share a joke or two. The pressure was off for them!

It worked. This was I believed a much better approach to selling to the client. When the other sales reps would be having their long chats with their clients, the clients must have felt the pressure to buy at the end of the presentation the whole way through which actually put them on edge as they knew the prolonged chit chat was in a way a form of being sneaky or false.

One hour later I had completed my whole presentation. Most other sales reps hadn't even finished their bullshit up front 'chit chat'

I looked beyond my couple and signalled to a manager that we were ready to see some pricing. I had provisionally secured the deal. I caught the attention of a manager who looked over at me. He knew I was calling him for pricing and he didn't look too happy. I was the new kid on the block. He must have thought I had fucked something up or wasn't doing my job properly as I finished too early. I introduced the manager. He gave us the pricing on the unit my couple were interested in.

The manager then said "I will leave the price with you guys"…

"I don't think you need to leave it with us" I said to the manager,

"I'm sure Mr & Mrs….are happy to proceed at that price".

You see, I had already pre emptied pricing with them and I knew what they would say yes to which they had agreed. The deal was agreed immediately. The manager completed the paperwork with them. The couple soon went to what we called 'The Button Up' room where the final paperwork would be completed with a 'back end' secretary.

I went back to the room where sales reps would wait to be called in for their next presentation.

"How did you get on" one guy said to me.

Another guy replied, "Probably not that great, he's only been in there for an hour" the he smirked.

"Deal done" I said.

They thought I was messing with them to start with but then my manager walked in. "Well done mate, you done that pretty quickly" he said. I just shrugged my shoulders. I found it easy. No big deal.

The day ended. There were a few deals that evening. I believe about 3 in total which was ok but not great for an evening's work for the whole office. I got one of the deals so I was clearly buzzing and delighted.

Was it beginners luck?

Day after day I would do a deal. This was unprecedented. Some days I would do 2 or even as many as 3 deals. Within a week I was the superstar at the office. I literally had 30 other sales reps, many of which were much older than me wanting to know how I was doing so well. What was my secret? I really don't know. It was easy for me.

Gold and Diamond Star

In my first week I became a 'Gold Star' Sales Rep. This meant that I had achieved a deal every day for 5 days on the trot. Only 1 other Sales Rep at our office had achieved this 'Honour'. There were 1 or 2 managers that had never achieved it!

So over the next few weeks I was absolutely smashing it. Deal after deal. The morning after the previous day's sales there would be a meeting. It was like additional training and motivation sessions. They would also give out something which were called 'Spifs' I think it stood for Special Performance Incentive funds. This was extra cash money that would be giving to a Sales Rep for any deals that they would achieve on that day.

On one particular day I completed 3 sales. This was almost unheard of. The incentive funds for that day happened to be massive. Each time a sale was done a manager will ring a bell on the sales floor so that the other potential clients that were being presented to could see that there were other customers buying timeshares which would hopefully entice them to do so also.

That afternoon/evening the bell rang 3 times for me. Each time the bell would ring they would shout out the Sales Reps name and the name of the couple. It was crazy, all day you could hear my name being shouted out "Spyros, Spyros, Spyros"!

It was a buzzing feeling. I was the cream of the Crop. That next morning, I took around £500 in cash for the 'Spifs' award. That would be on top of my 10% commission that I would earn for each sale. I made around £2000 that day. Back then that would have been how much a top level Premier League footballer would have earned in a day.

Within around 4 or 5 weeks I had achieved the 'Diamond Star' status. This was completing a deal a day for 10 days on the trot. This was unheard of. I believe that I was the only person in the UK to achieve such a target.

It got to the stage that I would be instructing my own managers on what to do. For example, after a while I knew very quickly after meeting a couple if they were going to buy from me. I usually gave it about 10 minutes. If I wasn't feeling it I would call my manager over and tell them that the couple were not suited to the product. We would then allow the couple to go after 10 minutes with their Free Gift in hand.

If I said there was no deal to be had, then there was no deal to be had. No argument about it. The managers wouldn't question me. I was the only Sales Rep in the office that had the power to do this.

Party Time

Two of the managers working there at this time were Hughie and Billy. They were in their mid-forties. They were two tough Glaswegians that loved a party.

One night we decided to go out clubbing. The club was called Middlesex and Herts and was a great pick up joint for older birds.

We had a good night and got on well with a group of ladies. They were invited back to Hughie's apartment for an after party.

Good after party. I leave it to your own imagination as to what happened. Anyway the next morning, everyone was still at the apartment and it was suggested that the party should keep going.

The Cocaine was ordered and the 2 Glaswegians and I drove over to Waitrose to top up on food and alcohol for the on-going party.

We were all still a little pissed from the night before and were staggering around a bit. It was funny. So we were pushing a large shopping trolley around. Bill and Hugh were picking up bottles of champagne, vodka, salmon and expensive meats. Fuck me it got to a stage that the trolley was over flowing with quality product. There must have been over £500 to £1000 worth of stuff in that trolley.

"Bill" I said 'how the fuck are we going to pay for this'?

"Don't worry son, I've got this" he said. Thank fuck for that I thought as I really didn't want to lay out shit loads of money for all that stuff.

Of course when he said 'don't worry I've got this, I presumed he meant that he was paying for it....

So the trolley is now full and we are at the back of the supermarket. Bill is pushing the trolley. At the back of the supermarket there are 2 electric doors. I don't know if they were entrances or exits. Bill walks straight towards the doors. The doors open and out we go!

Close to £1000 worth of food and drink had just been openly stolen from the supermarket. Bill and Hugh laughed. They had obviously pulled this rouse off before. I was a little scared. They didn't tell me what they were about to do. Probably best I didn't know. I was worried that we get caught on camera. Maybe we did but they couldn't identify who we were.

Needless to say when we got back to the apartment the ladies were very impressed with our shopping spree and were flattered that we spent so much money on treating them!!

Flanesford Priory

So I carried on working at the office in Borehamwood for around 3 months in total. I was then given the opportunity to go and work 'on site' at a place called 'Flanesford Priory' on the English and Welsh borders. It was the same job however the only difference being was that I was actually working at the site of an actual timeshare. Flanesford Priory was a very typically English kind of accommodation. It was an old Priory that had been modernised to create holiday homes. This kind of place would have been especially of interest for travelling Americans. It had a powerful position with regards to its strength in the RCI exchange system. On that basis the timeshares would or at least should have been very beneficial to their owners. It was a real archetypal Historic British residence/priory.

I worked there for a few months. It was great fun. Most nights the staff would go out for drinks and something to eat. On one particular night we appear to have ventured too far into Wales. We arrived at a small quaint village. There was about five of us guys on this particular occasion. We stopped off at a pub for drinks. It was a proper local's pub though. Everyone knew everyone. When us 5 guys went in there was the stereotypical scenario of where the pub goes quiet and everyone is looking at you because you are strangers. Seriously, they were looking at us as if we were fucking Aliens. Anyway we kept ourselves to ourselves in our little corner. After a pint or 2 we decided it would be best to leave the pub as it was a little tense in there due to our presence.

We got back in the car to leave the pub. We noticed that a group of Welsh lads had left the pub just moments after us. They got in their car. We were driving down the road, one way then another. We soon all realised "those Welsh Fuckers are following us". We then sped up, they would then speed up. They came right up our arse. Our driver, Adrian, a big Northern Rugby player decided we should stop the car and front them. I think most of us were a little scared as all of those Welsh fuckers were massive. We had to front them though.

Adrian got out of the car. Then we followed. The Welsh car stopped behind us. They got out of their car and walked over to us.

"What's up lads" Adrian says to the Welsh boys.

One of them steps forward and says "we are a bit annoyed, you see". "You were in our local pub and it seemed like you were taking the piss out of us"

We looked at each other – we didn't fucking do or say anything untoward. It continued like this for a while, backwards and forwards to one another. I was ready for it to kick off. I was sure we were going to get battered. Overall they were much bigger than us. However for some reason Adrian then said to their front man. "If we are going to have a row then we don't all need to get involved. It could turn out very nasty"

Adrian then looks at who we presumed was their top boy and said- "why don't just me and you have it out and whatever happens we can call it a day and move on". That was a fucking result I thought – I'm not going to get my head kicked in!

The Welsh guy looks at Adrian for a few seconds. He then raises his hand to Adrian to shake it. The Welsh guy says "I respect that mate – let's just leave at that and part our own ways".

Now, I don't think that the Welsh guy bottled it at all. I think that he knew that Adrian was just trying to save the arses of his mates. The Welsh guy I believe rated him for that so he put an end to it.

We got back in the car. They went their way and we went ours. Adrian turned to the 4 of us and says "You lucky fucking bastards" I just saved you from a proper beating. There was no doubt about it. He fucking did. Anyway Adrian, if you ever read this book then thanks once again lol.

I had been at 'Flanesford Priory' for a few months and I was getting itchy feet again. I decided to move over to Tenerife in Spain to work on an on-site accommodation. Once again it was the same sort of thing but being actually present on the site. This was the site that I used to sell when I started back in Borehamwood some 6 months earlier. So I knew all about the resort etc

I had only spent a few weeks there when I realised that there were better opportunities within the industry. I moved to a new Company down the road called 'Hollywood Mirage'.

They knew my track record there and welcomed me to the force. Now the Sales guys that were working at the Hollywood Mirage were on a different level to the ones I had previous worked with. They were the like me, the best of the best. Sales guys working there could easily earn up to £200,000 in a year. This was 1995 so that was bucket loads of money.

It was time to play with the big boys! I started off really well done a few deals. However after a week or so I started to go off the boil. I couldn't concentrate and my heart was just not in it anymore. I don't know why this happened. I think I got lazy and just wanted to be over there on holiday rather than sit in the sun all day trying to sell people timeshare. I must have only been there for about 6 weeks. I left. Shortly after that I came back to England.

I took a few months chilling out and then I got another job working for local newspapers. The Tottenham Journal was one of the papers, amongst others. This was based in Crouch End in North London. I had just been earning good money for the last 6 months. I don't know why I packed it in. Did I get bored of the work? When I look back I really can't put my finger on why I left.

So working for the local Newspapers was a big downwards step based against the financial opportunities that I had in Timeshare.

I knew working at the local papers was just a stop gap for me until I found the next exciting opportunity.

I believe that I worked there for less than a year and then I quit. I was getting bored. I needed something different. I needed a new challenge. I needed to earn big money again.

The call from James that changed my life -1996

So I had known James for a month or so by now. He was advertising sales work in the London Evening Standard. I met with him in Central London. We started off offering rentals in high valued apartments mostly in South West London…. However this didn't really work out well.

A couple of weeks later, we were about to go our own separate ways when James called me… "Sorry mate" I said 'doesn't look like it's worked out'… James had other ideas …. He said that he had come across something that involved selling Bordeaux Fine Wine as an investment…I wasn't really that interested… but the more he spoke about it the more intrigued I became. I was really very close to ending the call and leaving it at that but in the end I decided to meet up with him again to discuss this new potential opportunity further.

That call literally changed the pathway of the next 25 years of my life… it was 50/50 that nothing would have materialised from the call. I wonder where I would be in my life now had I not pursued with him and wine investment.

So I met with James. He had all of the information with him. I looked through it all and I was wowed by. Here was a great investment that had a 300 year track record of super amounts of profits being made. Why was no one else offering this opportunity I thought? With further investigation I realised this was quite a hush, hush investment opportunity where only the rich and famous new about it.

We studied the market place for a few days and realised this was an investment opportunity that could be introduced to the main stream investor. This was an 'alternative' investment opportunity and did not have to be FCA regulated.

We began the process of creating a website and brochures for our new company which was to be 'fronted' by a friend of James named 'Shane'

Little did we know at that time that we were one of the Protagonists to the creation of a £1 Billion Monster.

Bordeaux Fine wine Investment

Bordeaux Fine Wine Investments are the most investment worthy wine investments throughout the world. This is because Bordeaux is said to produces the greatest and finest wines in the world.

There is also a 300 year track record and tradition within certain Chateaux where the rich and famous like to procure the best wines from the best vintages.

The most famous and investment worthy wine producing Chateau from the region include, Margaux, Lafite Rothschild, Haut Brion, Latour, Mouton Rothschild, Petrus and Le Pin.

Traditionally there are maybe a further 20 investment wines from the region but the above detailed ones are the main ones.

Now, each Chateau produces around 20,000 to 30,000 cases of wine per year. There are usually 12 bottles within a case.

The quality of the harvest or vintage is determined by the weather for that particular year. If the weather produces perfect conditions then you have a good or great vintage. The wines are tasted early in within their production. The wine sits in barrels for a couple of years to allow them to mature before bottling. At the barrel stage the wines are known as 'En Primeur'. Tastings are conducted by the world's most respected critics and they generally score wines out of a 100. Therefore a high score early on within the life cycle of a wine could be the news that the wine/vintage for a particular wine could be great.

With further tastings of each individual wine at the En Primeur stage and further tastings after bottling, the wine can increase in value substantially as demand outstrips supply for the best of wines.

Wine is deemed to be a 'wasting asset' meaning that its life expectancy is no more than about 50 years. Therefore on that basis it classified as a Capital Gains Tax free investment. You could see why investors became very interested with the opportunity.

House of Lonroes

So the first wine investment business was set up. This was named 'The House of Lonroes' We had a small sales force in place, brochures printed, the website was up and running, accounts with Government Bonded Warehouses in the UK were set up to store the wine once the wine had been bottled and transferred to the UK from France.

All we had to do now is sell the wine. The wine would be for the main part purchased from 2 or 3 of the major wine merchants and brokers in the UK. Indeed the largest market for Bordeaux wine at the time was in the UK and not France. You could not purchase the wine direct from the Chateau in Bordeaux. You had to be something called a 'Negociant' to do this. There were very few 'Negociants' and most of those worked for the major wine brokers and merchants.

Investors loved the opportunity and the money was flying in. We then had a separate and larger sales office opened.

The House of Lonroes accumulated hundreds of client and millions of pounds of turnover. The business was doing really well but we then had a visit from the DTI (Department of Trade and Industry). The investigation didn't submit that we were doing anything illegal but their concern was that we were charging prices that were too high.

Unlike stocks, shares and gold etc where there is a fixed price that people buy and sell at.

With fine wine there is no such thing as a fixed price. One broker may sell a case of wine for £3000 another might sell at £3500 and another at £4000. It depends on what mark-up they want to achieve which is based on what they purchased the wine at in the first place.

Now major merchants and brokers generally sold their Bordeaux wine stock for a 'Retail consumption' item rather than an investment opportunity. On that basis you could understand how prices could vary. However we were selling the wines for Investment purposes only. The wine would be stored for the client in a government bonded warehouse and bought and sold there. The client would never actually even see the wine. They would just receive a certificate from the bonded warehouse once a wine had been put in their name.

The problem that the DTI had was not that we were selling wine as an investment as such but the price we were selling each case was on the higher range of pricing. Their theory being is that how were clients supposed to make money if the price that they were paying on the front end was already high.

I agree with this. Our prices back then was too high. However every client received their case or cases of wine in Bond with their certificates of ownership delivered.

Although our prices were high I believe that most if not all of those original clients would still have made a decent profit over the medium to long term.

So although we had some problems back then all was good in reality. However internal concerns on the model of the business including pricing caused some issues amongst us. It was decided that The House of Lonroes would close down and another business would arise that would benefit our clients moving forwards.

In about 1998 we also opened an office in Amsterdam then soon after we switched to Nice.

This had nothing really to do with wine investment but a couple of my mates who were working in the wine business at the time started to look at other business opportunities and preferred a life abroad. I would fly out there on occasion and see them. I think that this was the process that really kicked started my mind into wanting to live abroad. I didn't believe that Amsterdam or Nice where the right fit but something was brewing in my mind.

So having worked at the House of Lonroes for a couple of years it was time to move on.

Selling wine as an investment was a financially rewarding and interesting way to make a living with the financial rewards being potentially quite high.

Princess Diana

During the period that the House of Lonroes was running, I lived for about 1.5 years on Earls Court Road. It was a large house that a few of us rented privately. It was a great location and plenty of shops and bars along there.

The house that we lived in was one house away from where the commercial shops started. The first premises were a private gym that Princess Diana used to attend. The gym entrance was about 20ft away from the house I was living in. I saw the Princess on a couple of occasions walking into the gym. On one occasion I remember her passing me on the way to the gym …"Morning princess" I said. She looked at me smiled and blushed and walked in.

What a lovely lady I thought.

Horrifically a short period after she died in that tragic accident.

I do wonder what great things she could have achieved for our world, had she still been alive. It was such a waste and a shame. The thing that made it even worse was the circumstances surrounding the accident. Who knows what really happened.

I met Ann in 1997 at The Epping Forest Country club

It was May 1997 and I had been living in Earl's Court for about 6 months and working at our offices on Oxford Street at The House of Lonroes. Shane, Tim and I decided to go out clubbing to the Epping Forest Country Club. This was closer to where I was from and where Tim lived. Tim had just started working with us at the wine company and he lived in the Essex area.

The Epping Forest Country Club back in the day was very famous. It was also synonymous with persons from the Essex underworld. It was so popular in fact that if you dropped a bomb on the club on a given night you could wipe out half the Essex underworld in one swoop. It was the sort of place that the so called 'Essex Boys' would quite regularly frequent. These guys were probably the most notorious gangsters in Essex at the time. However they were murdered around 2 years earlier in a shooting.

So that night we were dancing away and I noticed a lady wearing a very pretty dress. She caught my attention and we started dancing. Well that person was Ann who I ended up marrying and is the mother to my 2 daughters. We would see each other a few times a week until we moved in together and she almost straight away thereafter got pregnant with our first daughter Sophia. You will read more about my family later on.

Beau Vin – 1998-1999

I worked with a friend in a new Wine Investment company that he set up after the termination of the House of Lonroes. This was for a couple of years from about 1998-1999.

Once again this was a successful company. The company was called Beau Vin – this is an Anglicism from French meaning Beautiful Wine. All wine had been purchased that was sold to clients and I am sure that the clients of this company would have made good profits in the medium term as the up-front margins that we were charging were much lower than those of the House of Lonroes.

This company was formed with my best mate 'Tim' who would also be my best man at my wedding some years later. We went to Spurs together, clubbing and working together. For those few years we were like brothers.

The company traded for 2 or so years but it was time for me to move on.

However, during this time, Tim, Ryan and Christopher that worked with me took a short break to Iceland.

That was close

We were back at Iceland's main airport after a nice few days trip to this quite amazing northern hemisphere country. The weather was mental. Snow, blizzards, ice, fog the lot! We were sitting in the airport and you could clearly see the view of the outside. "There's no bloody way we are going anywhere" I said to the others… they agreed…

"Fuck going on a plane in this weather"…Ryan said. Whilst we were chatting over what to do next they called our flight to the departure lounge…

"They are having a laugh" Tim said….anyway we went to the departure lounge where we met all the other people going on our flight.

Everyone was questioning if the flight should be going ahead under these atrocious weather conditions. We got on the plane… people were nervy….we very slowly moved round the runway which seemed like an eternity…then we were off… the plane was shaking… the turbulence was the worst I ever felt… this is going to be a fucking disaster I thought… the worst bit was when the plane felt like it would suddenly drop 100ft… sort of like you were on the downside of a rollercoaster. Everyone had to remain buckled up for the whole flight… young children crying all the way due to turbulence…seriously many people sat motionless in their seats and some were praying… why the fuck was the chance taken to fly this plane in these conditions… people were scared but also angry… one lady starting shouting at one of the air stewardesses 'whose fault is it if we die' now that didn't make things any bloody better. That flight was 2 of the scariest hours of my life… I still can't believe how we were allowed to fly.

Trip to Bordeaux

I believe it was in 2000 that Ann – and my daughter Sophia who was barely 2 at the time took a Trip to Bordeaux to visit the various Chateaux and to learn more about the most famous wine region in the world. This market place was to be my career so I wanted to know as much about it as I could.

I already had close to 4 years' experience in the market place, and new everything that I needed to know. I had help set up and run other successful wine companies. It was time to set up my own wine investment business

By 2000 I had sold my house in Edmonton some years earlier …at a loss and also sold a flat that I bought In Southgate also some years earlier to fund the purchase of a new family home in Billericay in Essex.

We wanted to get out of London and Essex was the main choice of area as Ann is originally from Westcliffe on Sea. So we had a small 3 bedroom house. Sophia was a toddler so all good.

My First Office - Next to St Pauls Cathedral

I rented an office Next to St Pauls Cathedral in the City. My first wine business was born. It was called Bordeaux Wine Consultants. The business was me and a couple of other sales people. We were raking in the deals. The same process and set up as before. It continued on like this for about a year. I had obtained over 100 client's at the time and turned over 1 Million pounds before I had reached my 30th birthday. I decided though that I had enough clients and I could just service them and continue with a good yearly income by myself on that basis.

I gave up the office in London and converted my garage back at home to an office and would continue working from there.

Depression

I eventually turned over £2M which was good. All clients received their wine up to then and good profits were being made for those clients……However, by the time we got to about 2003 I was becoming very depressed and lazy due to this depression. I hated working, I had lost all desire. I would spend most of the day lying on the couch. I would sleep for hours on end. I was losing track of my business, the business had dramatically slowed down due to my inability to operate due to my never ending depressive state. I felt like I had no worth or purpose in life. I was losing the will to live. The only thing that could escape me from those feelings was to go out once a week and get drunk and take cocaine. I used to count the days down until the weekend when I would then go out and temporarily relieve the depression I was feeling.

Up until the depression started the business was doing just fine but for the forthcoming year starting in late 2003 I lost track of what I was doing. I was overspending, forgetting to order wine, making mistakes about which client bought which wine. My brain became frazzled.

I had to escape and find a way out of this horrendous depression. I couldn't continue living the way I was living. In April 2004 we found out that Ann was pregnant with our second daughter to be – Elena. I started investigating the possibilities of moving abroad. I needed a change of life, and a different surrounding. I spoke to Ann about it. She wasn't sure at first but the agreed we could give it a go. I identified Marbella in Spain to be the place that would suit us best. There were great English Schools and things to do for the whole family etc. Within a week of coming up with the idea of moving abroad, we agreed and I started looking for accommodation to rent to get us started over there.

My Big Fat Greek Wedding

I believe the thing that pissed me off the most when it comes to family was the day of my wedding. I had to organise the whole thing by myself… ok fair enough but what really pissed be off is that a lot of my family knew this. Now a couple of my uncles were the nearest thing to me having parents. It's Ann and my big day and I wanted things to run smoothly… but it didn't help when some of the family arrived to the church late. Would they have arrived late if it was the wedding for one of their own kids? - No chance.

I mean over the years there is a lot more I can say about various situations that my sister and I felt let down by…but it goes to show that just because some family members gave it the large that they cared for me and my sister… well they were just empty words and when it came to the crunch of them doing something or should be doing something, well in reality they did fuck all.

The wedding went really well. There was lots of Greek food and dancing. Ann and I got thousands of pounds pinned on us. This is a tradition at a Greek wedding

Marbella

Just 1 month after we got married and by the beginning of August we had moved to Marbella.

Marbella is on the south Eastern coast of Spain. It is probably Europe's version of Miami. You will find many celebrities and rich there but also crime ridden with drug gangs importing drugs in mostly from Africa then transferred to other parts of Europe.

Anyway, this was all achieved within 4 months of first having the idea to moving abroad.

We lived in a large Townhouse on quite an exclusive complex with a beautiful communal swimming pool.

Bordeaux Wine Consultants was still running. I was feeling as little better. The ability to go to the beach a couple of times a week along with the holiday culture feeling gave me that new burst of energy that I very much needed. However, although the business was still running, I managed to finally realise that I had made mistakes that had left the business £100,000 plus in debt. This debt was mainly owed to clients. That period of depression back in England caused me to make some right old fuck ups. Technically the company was insolvent.

There were clients waiting for some of their wines. These were En Primeur wines – which had been sitting in the barrel at the Independent Chateau in France for the last couple of years and had now been bottled. Therefore the client would expect that their case/s of wine would by now have been delivered to the UK Bonded Warehouse. These En Primeur wines are where the mistakes I made were mainly focused on.

I couldn't deliver the wines. I could find no way out of the situation so legally I had to liquidate the company. However it is important to note that maybe a small percentage of clients lost some of their wine stock, however overall they still would have financially benefitted. The wines that had been delivered were great investment wines and even those 20 clients or so that lost some of their wine due to my mistakes would have ended up with more money than they started with as the wines they did hold appreciated in value considerably that outweighed any losses.

So the business was liquidated and I was banned as a Director of a UK Limited company for 12 years.

The depressive side of my Bi Polar Disorder - which still had not been diagnosed at that stage, was Key in the ultimate failing of the business.

Let the Chaos Begin – Life changer

Oh dear…..what happens from now on is for the most part a disaster! However, being where I am now and after taking into account what happens here in my story over the next 20 years to bring me to where I am today, i believe that my encounters with superior Alien beings which you will read about later on, will bring some substance and meaning to my rollercoaster of a life.

Now prepare yourself for the rest of my story…

Marbella Madness – Staring 2004 – 2005
Shooting number 1

I had only been living in Spain for a couple of months or so. I was on a night out in Premier club which was a striper's bar above Linekers bar on the second line Puerto Banus.

It wasn't a big place but a good place to start your evening off. Both men and women used to go there and it would be a good little atmosphere. So one night I'm standing by the bar chatting with a girl… ok stripper…then suddenly I heard what initially sounded to me like Chinese fire cracker noises.

People started screaming and running out of the bar. I looked down and literally just a few feet away from me was a guy lying on the ground. He had been shot multiple times. I didn't know if he was dead … people were streaming out of the bar.

There were always police around the bar areas so I knew I had to get out of there quickly. To be there when the police arrived could have been long and problematic to me for numerous reasons. I got out went downstairs and into Linekers bar. I got a drink and sat there for a minute and pondered. The guy that had been shot was standing literally a few feet away from me. Even a slightly stray bullet could have hit me…. Fuck me that was close. It was obviously a gang related shooting. That was the first of many gun related incidents I was exposed to over the years to come.

Sometime later, I heard that the man had been smoked. You know… killed.

What were the chances of me being in the middle of a shooting, I thought - after only being in Marbella for 2 months. I didn't want to see that again….once again oh dear…you will have to read on!

Land banking

There was a new kind of investment arriving on the scene. It was called Land Banking. This is where Land that did not have planning permission in the UK would be identified. However the Land would be deemed as having good prospects of receiving planning permission for homes at a later date. Companies were buying large plots of land that they deemed could eventually receive planning permission. The land would be divided into plots. The plots would then be sold to private investors at a price with a view that when that land obtained planning permission the value of that land would dramatically increase.

On that basis I opened up a small office in Marbella to act as a Sales agency for the Land Banking business that was situated in the UK. My friends Tim and Mark from England came over and joined my sales operation. It was going quite well for a year but the main office in the UK was coming across many legal problems which entail caused problems for us getting paid what we were owed. About a year after I started the sales operation I closed it down as we could not rely on the future of the opportunity.

Birth of my daughter Elena - School and Parties

Elena was born right at the End of 2004. I now had 2 beautiful daughters. Sophia was already attending school in 2004 and by 2006-2007 so was Elena.

My daughters went to Aloha International College. It was a great school in a lovely area. It is a private school. Many of my daughter's friends had very rich parents… Multi-Millionaire's.

Funny enough my eldest daughters best friend was the daughter of Vinny Samways that played for Tottenham Hotspur in the 1990s… anyway just like we do over here in England most kids have birthday parties. So on one occasion we were invited to a party of one of the girl's friends. We pulled up to a massive villa on the Golden Mile strip… it was decorated with birthday bits on the outside… looked very nice. Anyway we walked through to the back garden which was the size of a football pitch… 'Fuck me' they had hired an entire fairground for the party… seriously it was an entire bloody fare. There were bumper cars, rides and all the other stuff, first class food and drinks, chocolate fountain machines, servants and Disney characters… the party must have cost at least £20,000… this was for a 6 year old child.

Drowning – Not Again!

So I don't know whether what happened next was at this party but a similar party. So Elena would have been aged I guessing at 1.5 years old. So she was walking and even running a little. She had been in swimming pools many times as were always surrounded by them. Elena went off with Sophia and a group of other girls outside to enjoy the party. A little while later, Ann went to look for the girls to see how they were getting on.

Five minutes later Ann comes back. She is crying and holding Elena in her arms. What the fuck is going on I thought. Elena was crying also. "She almost drowned" shouted Ann tearfully. Apparently Elena got separated from the other girls in the enormous back garden and somehow made her way around to the side of the villa where the swimming pool was. Elena must have jumped in. There was no one else there. Ann spotted her. Elena was drowning and trying to grab hold of the edge of the pool. Ann ran over to her and scooped her out.

We can't say for sure but if Ann didn't decide to go for that walk until 2 minutes later if at all then the chances are my little guy would have drowned. Can you just imagine that? Ever since then and even though now both my daughters are adults, Ann and I are extremely wary and cautious of whatever Sophia and Elena are doing. This event still leaves me a little traumatised as I know how close to disaster the event could have been.

New wine companies 2006

So the Land Banking business had finished and I had to find new work. I had noticed that the Bordeaux Fine Wine Investment market was really bullish at this time. I didn't think I would ever get back into it. I ended up fucking up the last wine business. However, I didn't actually lose any one any money in real terms. As explained above even though there was some wine stock not delivered, overall with the wine that was delivered those clients that had lost out on the small percentage of wine that was not delivered would have made that money back from their investments that were fulfilled.

I was feeling better now than before when I was in a depressive state in England so I thought I had the right morally and fairly to give the wine investment business another go.

I set up a Spanish company called Alpha Invest Worldwide. The company was to sell Spanish property and Bordeaux Fine Wine as an investment. Brochures and a website were created. An office was opened up and away I went. By 2006 I was fully operational. I had the small office in Spain and a larger sales office in London that was run by a friend that I had previously worked with.

Wine Deals were coming in fast over those first few months. I started off by selling non En-Primeur wine i.e wine that was older that had already been bottled and cased and often was already sitting In Bond in the UK where a simple transfer of ownership would be done from a previous owner of the case of wine to my client that had purchased the wine.

By the middle of 2006 I was becoming a little stressed and anxious. I think the start of alcohol and cocaine abuse was getting to me physically and mentally.

I went to see my doctor in Marbella that prescribed me strong anti-depressants and anti-stress pills. This is where the real disaster kicks in. At this time it was still not known that I suffered with Bi

Polar Disorder. If you have Bi Polar Disorder you are not supposed to take strong medication for anxiety and stress etc. In doing so this would instigate episodes of mania within Bi Polar sufferers. Mania is another word for Psychosis

Unfortunately for me and everyone else the manic episodes I would proceed to suffer were constant over the next 6 years that sent my mind and my life into chaos…..

I was taking these medications all the way through the running of the wine businesses … no wonder my manic episodes were out of control and caused the things I done within the business to be done.

£50,000 or bust

One day, the whole of the Marbella office were waiting for their monthly wages. About 15 people in total. The money I was expecting to come in hadn't and I had overloaded on wine purchases. Employees were starting to get stressed and I was in a tricky situation. All hell would have broken loose if I did not sort out their money. Ex pats in Marbella mostly live day to day financially, so if they didn't get their money in the next 24 hours they would be fucked.

However there was a client that had ordered £50,000 of stock and was due to pay by that day. It was time to call him! The whole office sat there in anticipation but with some anger… hoping that I could get the money in that day from the deal.

I called the client…. "How are you sir" etc etc…apparently he had read something on a website called investdrinks.org that put my company in a negative light. The sight was and still is run by a Canadian chap called Jim Budd. He is a journalist that writes on all things wine and has a special section for those companies that acted differently to the norm within the marketplace and that he thought were unscrupulous! The article he wrote I believed stated that the price of wine that I was charging was too high etc etc.

Somehow I managed to turn the client round and he paid that day. I was on the phone with him for about an hour with my staff eagerly watching.

That was a close one!

So 1 year into the business things started slowly getting out of hand. During this period we were selling cases of wine so fast that by the time a client made an order and we had received the money the price of the case had increased and this started causing a bit of a mess. In one instance I think it was the Lafite Rothschild 2005 or 2006 vintage almost doubled in price in one day…it was getting out of control.

It was around this time I truly realised that there was something wrong with me mentally…..

Addicted

We are now moving well into 2006.

I was starting to drink excessively and snorting cocaine. When I went out at night I couldn't stop the drinking and the snorting, I would keep going until 7am or even later that next morning. I would be getting home when my kids were getting ready for school. It was embarrassing for me. I hated myself, why was I doing this? I was drinking enough alcohol in those sessions for 3 nights out. The cocaine kept me going all night. I was addicted. I would then spend the next 2 or 3 days recovering and once I had recovered I would go out and do the same thing again and again and again. However there is a lot more to this which you will read later.

Son of God Part 1

It was an afternoon at the weekend. My sister was living with me at the time. She had come over for a few months break from her banking work. She wanted to explore something different.

There was a group of us in Linekers bar for the Saturday afternoon Premier league football on TV. This was always a busy time. The bar was quite packed.

I don't really have a memory of what I did next and why but my sister recorded it on her mobile phone.

I was having a manic episode. I stood on one of the tables and was preaching in a very strange and loud way that I was the 'Son of God' and I was here to save the poor children of the world.

My sister was later in tears and showed me the video… what the fuck!! OMG how embarrassing… I looked like I was in a trance and mumbling very quickly but also shouting I could barely understand myself… this went on for a good few minutes before I was brought down from the table. I don't know what happened then and what the time line was before in effect I became sane again.

Although my sister had previously suspected that there was something wrong with me mentally she had never witnessed a manic episode of bi polar which clearly scared her. That's mainly because since the accident we had almost always lived apart.

At the time we still did not know it was bi polar disorder - in fact I'm not even sure at the time I knew what bi polar was but it was going to get a lot worse over the forthcoming years.

It is difficult to explain what it is like when you are in a manic state of bi polar disorder. This is partly due to the fact that one can enter into psychosis and therefore not really know or even remember what they have done or how they have acted.

I know that when I am in a manic episode I can go into a daze, almost trance like situation that can last for hours… I am fully awake and could be sitting or lying down… my mind would create spectacular innovative and complex plans or ideas where in one episode I have within my mind clearly solved (as I would be aware) immediately the cure for poverty or starvation. I would also create ideas that could make a business grow to a £100 million value in months. The idea would come to me in pieces like a puzzle and I would fit them all together perfectly and come up with a solid concept that I had no doubt would work. This would happen time and time again.

However my mind started changing in other ways. I was becoming more aggressive and violence started appearing in my character. I am not a violent person and never have been. It's just not me.

Meeting Alexander Dembinski

So anyway, my new wine company had been running for some months and one of my staff was a lady called Julia. She was a well-educated Russian lady that had many Russian contacts in the Marbella area. She was running a concierge service as part of a wider wing of the company. The concierge service focused on wealthy Russians. It is through this avenue that she met Alexander Dembinski and then introduced him to me.

Alexander was quite a well-known business man in the area. He dealt in various investments and claimed to have contacts all over Europe that could source investment opportunities and at the best prices.

Alexander is a tall man… maybe 6ft 4inches I would say. He was always immaculately dressed and groomed. You would often see him in the port area at restaurants having meetings etc.

So when I met him for the first time his face was quite familiar. He stated that he had one or two friends that were from Switzerland that were 'negociants' for the top Chateaux in Bordeaux. He stated that he was able to purchase wines cheaper than the normal market price.

We chatted for a while. I believed everything he told me and had no reason not.

I started ordering En Primeur stock from him. That is wine that is still in the barrel and had not been bottled as of yet.

He would provide me with invoices. I would pay him in cash or bank transfers … but mostly cash as he said he could get slightly better deals on cash transactions.

The fine wine market was at a stage where it was the most 'bullish' it had been in its 300 year history.

I would buy £5000 of stock one week and more the next week etc etc.

Ultimately over the next couple of years I purchased hundreds of thousands of pounds of wine stock from him.

So it was around 2 years after meeting with him for the first time and making my first purchase that I was due to start receiving some of the now bottled stock from him. I believe it was stock from the 2005 vintage. This was one of the greatest vintages in history.

However, it was 2008 now and Alexander apparently started running into some problems. He was not able to fulfil the orders. He delayed and delayed... eventually I got a little scared of the situation. However to compensate me for the delay and to reassure me he started handing back lump sums of cash to me. In those next few months he handed back around £40,000 of cash to me.

However he owed a lot more than that to me. Unfortunately this was just the beginning of the problem. You will read more about what happened over the next couple of years further down the time line of my book.

With regards to Julia and her husband Ernesto I ended being best man at their wedding. They were good friends of mine and helped me out on various situations. I have lost contact with them but the last I heard was that Julia was seriously Ill and they were planning to move to Mexico to enjoy what little time Julia has left.

Dancing with the Gods

By now I was living a life of partying to the extreme. I was out all of the time. I was out of control. Most of my nights would be spent dancing hours on end.

Dance silhouette - when I dance I am on a journey. It is a spiritual movement of grandiosity that gives me closeness with the universe. I have never seen anyone that remotely dances like I did. Now it is important that you understand that my dancing was not a gesture of superior dancing skills. My dancing was a euphoric silhouette to the greatness of our superior beings.

The dance style uses mostly my arms to express a greatness and philosophy.

Whenever and wherever I danced it would always attract a crowd. People couldn't believe it. I would have men and women saying that my dancing was amazing and they had never seen anything like it. Several people over the years said it was almost like I would be telling a profound and powerful storey.

One lady that was a professional dancer stated that I was the best male dancer she had ever seen.

However I do remind you that in fact I was not the best male dancer she had ever seen. I was maybe the most unique dancer she and others had ever seen.

I don't know where this journey of dance started for me but I realised a long time ago that I was sending out a message to others.

The message was that we must understand higher levels of life and being. I would in effect portray the greatness of superior beings within my movements.

I wanted people to understand the matrix of possibilities and that my method of dancing would express how being greater in oneself would eventually lead to a superior after life.

Irish dancing

I think that one of the best forms of expressive and silhouette dancing in the world and currently is Irish dancing. I feel that there is such power and meaning in the foot- steps and leg movements of this kind of dance. It clearly tells a powerful and emotional story.

This is the reason why it is so popular worldwide. The reason that I mention Irish dancing is that is the closest equivalent that I could come up with in the way I danced. The difference being is that with Irish dancing you use your legs mostly as the expressive figure of movement whereas when I danced it was my arms and hands that were the expressive symbols

I am sure you will have a better understanding when you see the film that will be based on this book.

Wayne Lineker - Dance off

So for those of you that don't know, probably mostly people outside of Europe that are reading this book, Gary Lineker was one of England's greatest ever football goal strikers. His brother is Wayne Lineker. Many years ago the brothers (mainly Wayne I think) set up a chain of bars, mainly in Spain. The bars are called Linekers bar. As I used to frequent Linekers bar in Puerto Banus very regularly, over a period of time I got to know Wayne. He is a real fun and funny guy. We often had a good laugh.

On one occasion at the bar, it was somehow decided that Wayne and I would have a 'dance off' on the middle of the dance floor in front of the hundreds of partying holiday makers.

It was a surreal moment... almost something like you would see in the movie Saturday night fever.

Wayne is a good dancer, I'm not sure who won but it was a buzzing moment not only for the two of us but also for our audience. I'm pretty sure Wayne will remember it.

Leaving Ann and the Kids

After another night of debauchery I got home at about 8am in the morning. I was fucked out of my head. I walked in and Ann looked at me like I was a disgrace. She started crying and shouting at me 'where the fuck have you been'. I can't take this anymore. The girls started crying. I was ashamed. They were on their way out somewhere. They stormed off. I lay down on the bed and I was crying. I hated myself and literally felt like I wanted to die. I couldn't do this to them anymore. What was wrong with me? Why could I not stop?

I had no time to recover so soon after I had to go to my office as we were open on Saturdays. My office manager 'Jane' had opened up. I arrived at the office.

"Look at the fucking state of you" Jane said to me.

"Have you even been home yet" she was pissed off with me even though I was her boss.

I started crying. I told her what happened earlier with the kids and Ann.

"Go home and sort your fucking self out" she said.

Jane was a lovely but tough Scouser (a person from Liverpool). She was a few years older than me and needed to give me a kick up the arse sometimes due to my behaviour.

I went home. Ann and the kids were still out. I knew I couldn't put them through my disgusting behaviour anymore but I also knew I could not trust myself to behave. I was addicted to so many things.

I lied down on the bed thinking about what the best solution would be. There was only one thing I could do at that moment in time. I had to leave the home and live somewhere else so that they would not suffer anymore.

Soon they arrived back home. I told Ann we had to talk. We sent the kids downstairs to play.

I told Ann that I was mentally fucked. I didn't know what I was doing half the time. She of course already knew this. She said I needed help. I was losing the plot. The kids could not see me like this anymore. I told her it was best that I left at least the foreseeable future until I sorted myself out. We both cried but both knew there was no other option.

That day I left. I rented an apartment elsewhere.

We didn't really tell the girls that I had moved out as such but just moving to a different apartment at that time. The girls were only 3 and 8 years old at the time so didn't fully understand and just got on with the new situation.

Ann and I never wanted my girls to see me in that fucked up state again.

So for the remaining 4 years that we lived in Spain we lived apart. This worked out for the best as the girls never saw me like that time again. I would still see them, 4 or 5 times a week.

After school, taking them to the beach etc etc. something had to be done and moving out was the only option. However it worked out for the better for my daughters as they didn't see their dad off his head on alcohol and drugs again.

Violent me?

I had been on the medication prescribed for over a year now. It was a typical evening and I went to this small bar on the 2nd line…there was a barmaid there I'd been talking to and we were getting on quite well … just having a drink at the bar…there was a couple towards the other end of the bar… clearly just trying to enjoy themselves on a night out. However I noticed this guy

◄ This is me at around 7 years old. By this age I had already been kidnapped, got caught up in an armed robbery and my mum almost died when crashing her car through a shop window.

This is me at 12 years old on the Greek Island of Kos where I caught fish and an Octopus with a child's fishing net! I also got stung by a jelly fish on this holiday. This was just 2 years before the tragic accident where both my parents died and I almost did also. ►

▲ This is me aged almost 20 years old in 1991 on Hollywood Boulevard whilst living in Los Angeles.

▲ Me and my friend Aydin on Hollywood Boulevard.

▲ Me as a holiday rep in corfu in 1994

◄ Some of the trophies that I won as a Timeshare sales legend.

▲ Me and my mates in the blue lagoon in Iceland in 1999

▲ Me and Mark outside the spurs ground in around the year 2000

▲   Me Tim and Mark at my 30th Birthday Party in 2001

Me at my Greek wedding
covered in money in 2004   ➤

◄   This is me holding a bottle of 'Petrus' which
is worth about £3000. This was on my visit to
Bordeaux in France

▲ This is a photo of the entrance of 'Chateau Petrus' in Bordeaux. This small production 'Garage' wine is one of the most expensive and sought after wines in the world.

◄ This is a photo of the entrance of Chateau 'La Mission Haut Brion' another one of the top wines that I sold as an investment that helped me turnover £10 million

▲ Me and my 2 daughters in the swimming pool in Marbella in 2007

▲ Me at Ocean Club in Marbella in 2006

◄ Me standing outside of my office with
the view of Marbella in the background

▲ This is a photo of Belmarsh prison. I spent 4 years in prison
for an apparent crime I didn't even know I had committed.

▲ Me in 2019 after my release from prison

▲ 'The Wild West Of Tottenham High Road' as a hobby I create unique cultural football designs. This is my one of Spurs…

I met 3 angels from another planet… they shared the words of God… I will share with you in this book not only the words they sent from God but the 500 shades of sex they communicated with me which will leave you absolutely blown away and not you would expect!

standing next to them that seemed a bit drunk. He kept making stupid comments to the couple and I could see that the couple were feeling very uneasy about the situation.

Anyway this guy kept on pestering them and became abusive to the couple who now looked a bit scared of the whole situation. I thought the guy in the couple who was 6ft 3 inches at least and being Irish would have turned to the idiot and told him to fuck off or lump him one right in the face… instead he sort of froze.

One of the bar maids asked me to get rid of the guy…. I went over to him and said 'time to leave mate' so he started abusing me in his South African accent'. I pulled the guy to the ground and dragged him outside… but he was still trying to fight his way back in… 'What a fucker'…. I sat on him and started punching his face… he was trying to fight back…. Blood started shooting out of his nose… by now there was a crowd round us watching including the Irish couple that he had been abusing.

I said to the big Irish guy "go on mate" give him a kick and so he did…2 police officers arrived and luckily the bar staff told them that the South African guy was the one that needed to be arrested and not me and that what happened.

What made me behave like this I do not know for sure but my brain had now really started to accelerate into all different directions. Although I have had a few minor scuffles or fights in my time there was nothing overly major that had ever caused me to act like that. However as time had gone on I started to get more aggressive.

Ocean Club

Well these were the days certainly before I totally lost the plot. It was a beautiful summer's day in Marbella at Ocean club. Ocean club was in effect a large outdoor swimming pool with a DJ, bar and restaurant. In peak season this placed was mobbed with party people. Everyone would be drinking bottles of champagne and sniffing the white stuff. There would be a good few hundred people at each party. It was an orgy of debauchery… people having sex in the toilets and even on some occasions on their sun beds in view of everyone. There was house and garage music banging out… it was mental… for most blokes and women this was the equivalent of heaven. I suppose it was for me also at the time but I don't really look back on those occasions with memory as participating in such events was part of the, in reality shocking life that I led at the time.

Now I wasn't famous but I was a bit of a face at the time in Marbella… lots of people new me… not because I was anyone special just I was on the scene for many years and many people got to know me whether it be ex pats living there or regular holiday makers to Marbella from the UK.

At one of the events, there was a group of us … all off our tits… the music was rocking. At each side at the top end of the pool were podiums. They were probably about 15ft off the ground. There was a professional dancer both male and female (usually both female though) dancing on each podium.

Now back then I was known for being a bit of a dancer. You will have read this in earlier pages. My mate Tim said to me… "Spyros why don't you get up there and dance"…. What a good idea I thought… lol!

I called one of the dancers to get down and so she did…. I went up…. The DJ saw me… he knew me from Linekers bar where he was a DJ. He gets on the microphone and announces … hey guys it's Spyros time. First my group of mates start cheering them the whole fucking club start cheering as I started my dancing routines… it was fucking buzzing and hilarious as people were shouting out 'Go on Spyros … go on my son fucking have it!! Lol

For the forthcoming years whenever I was out I would have random people come up to me that I didn't know that would say hey your 'Spyros the dancer'… yes I am! Fucking hilarious….

2nd shooting

So it was a typical weekend and the local bar was packed out as usual with all of the local ex- pats.

I was towards the back end of the beer garden. Suddenly i here bang, bang, bang coming from inside the bar… i straight away knew that there was a shooting going on. I looked towards the bar and one of my friends/acquaintances came pegging it out the bar running for his life. A small guy dressed all in black including a balaclava was just a few steps behind him chasing and shooting right at him… there were a couple more shots and my mate collapsed into a seating area just by an exit from the garden where the hit man escaped from.

'Fuck me' a load of us ran over. He had been shot many times. We thought he was going to die. The ambulance soon came along… ultimately he survived.

This was now the 2nd gun related incident i found myself in the middle of and this event actually started making me a little nervy of the Marbella scene as a whole.

Now the guy that got shot wasn't really a friend as such but more of an acquaintance of the higher echelons of the Marbella scene. To be one of these people you either had lots of money which I did at the time or were a gangster or a celebrity.

Gangster

Often we would see each other when we were out in bars or clubs and sit at the same table. Bottles of vodka and champagne would be flowing and we would be surrounded by women although admittedly some of those women would be Brazilian prostitutes…

Ok everyone knew who this guy was and without saying you could guess what his main trade was. When you are that close to someone you find out what it's really like to be a gangster. I tell you there is a lot of glamour but it must have been fucking scary. There are several main groups of gangsters in the Costa del Sol and they are involved in the same thing. If you fuck about with one group then you are putting your life at risk and you could be knowingly or even unknowingly a target at any time.

By now I would have been spotted with this guy and his firm on numerous occasions and it dawned on me after that night of the shooting that it was a possibility that I could somehow be targeted in a revenge attack or even be hit by a stray bullet if I was in the middle of a situation.

I think soon after I started realising how in all reality how I was living a shocking life and maybe soon it would be time to get out of Spain.

Scousers

Now as previously mentioned there were a few groups of gangsters on the Costa del Sol. I would say one of the more notorious or fearsome gangs were the Scousers. These guys were a very close nit community… they lived a few miles set back from the port in little 'urbanizations'/villages that also included trap houses. A trap house is mainly used for the cutting and distribution of drugs. You very rarely saw them or even knew who they were. They were smart.

On one occasion I was pissed up as usual I found myself up in a small bar which was embedded in a complex of apartments and villas in a small gated village like community. I don't know how the fuck I ended up there but it was late night or early hours of the morning.

I got myself a beer and sat down. Next to me were a group of 5 lads. Clearly Scousers and in my belief most certainly gangsters… you could just tell. I thought it best to keep myself to myself and pondered actually whether it was right for me to even be in there. Not that I was a problem or these lads would even give a shit but still you never know.

Now I'm well acquainted with the regional accents of the UK and have no problem understanding them. However I had never heard Scousers talk like this before. I literally could not understand a word they were saying not one… do Scousers have their own secret language that most of us do not know about lol?! I heard Steven Gerrard (famous Liverpool footballer) say on a jovial interview once that he speaks 2 languages English and Scouse… I know what he means now. Seriously I never heard anything like it…. Anyway I had a feeling that they were talking business so didn't stay long and got the fuck out if there.

Sir John Hall

I'm guessing it must have been around 2006 to 2007 that I bumped into Sir John Hall, the ex- owner of Newcastle Football Club. He was by himself early one Saturday afternoon in Lineker's bar. The bar was quite quiet at that time. He was having a pint…I stood at the bar, ordered my pint… I looked over at him and said "Sir John" …

"Yes how are you" he replied.

We started talking about football and we got to start talking about why he sold Newcastle. He said that with all the rich new foreign owners coming into the game that Newcastle would struggle to keep up. He said that he didn't have the funds to keep up with them so he knew it was time to pass the club on to a new owner.

I informed him I was a Spurs supporter. We then somehow got into the conversation of which was the bigger club ie Spurs or Newcastle… he made his point of view that it must be Newcastle as they got 52,000 coming to watch them every week whereas spurs only got 36,000. Sir John I said 'that's because your ground is bigger!! Are you s bigger club than Liverpool because your ground has a larger capacity I questioned… then I went through history and trophies and he knew I was winning the conversation… he smiled soon finished his pint. What a great 20 minutes or so meeting a Geordie legend that has done so much for his home town. Thank you Sir John it was a privilege meeting such a great man.

Celebrities

The amount of celebrities that visit Marbella is quite incredible. You could literally meet one every night.

I have met Ricky Hatton one of the UKs greatest ever boxers. It was quite strange actually. I was pottering around the outside of a bar. It was day time and I saw Ricky having a couple of drinks with his mates. He suddenly looks over at me and shouts out "hey Spyros"…

Strange I thought … how the fuck does Ricky Hatton know me. So I walked over …"hello mate" I said 'how are you…do you know me'?

"No" he said 'but everyone else around here seems to'.

Anyway we had a quick chat and a little banter. Good down to earth bloke… just one of the lads.

I've danced in a bar with the great Cilla Black, shared a drink with ex gangster David Courtney.

I have had a night out with Britain's most famous gangster over the last 20 years… I don't want to say his name. Let's just say he is a big Everton supporter.

I have chatted with footballer at the time and now TV pundit on the beach – Jermaine Jenas. It was funny because at the time he played for Newcastle. I was with my mate Mark at the time. We are both Spurs supporters. We were joking around with him and said why don't you come and play for Spurs. A few weeks later he signed for Spurs!?

I met Alan Davies. You know the actor with the big flop of curly hair that stars in Jonathan Creek. He is a big Arsenal fan.

I have also met ex-boxer - Prince Naseem Hamed, the late great Jade Goody and many more.

I caught a couple of other ex-footballers misbehaving but I won't mention any names. One was snorting cocaine and the other left a bar with a prostitute when I knew he was married at the time.

Simon Jordan

I met Simon on 4 or 5 occasions. For those of you that don't know, he is the ex-owner of Crystal Palace football club. I believe he owns a home in Marbella and spends much of his time over there. Simon is a very interesting and polite man. He always had time for a chat. I would usually bump into him at Nissi Beach or in a restaurant. He is a good bloke. I would like to meet up with him again one day. In the meantime keep up the good work on Talk Sport Simon…great entertainment

Samuel L Jackson

However the strangest situation is when I met with Samuel L Jackson!

It was a week night and a friend and I decided to pop out for a drink. The bar we went to although quite large, was on the golden mile and not where you expect to see many people on a week night. So anyway we sat down. I looked over at the over end of the bar. "Fuck me" I thought it's Samuel L Jackson.

I told my mate, a Swedish Chap that is called Niklas although for some reason I called him 'The Jackal'! He agreed it was Jackson.

What the fuck is Samuel L Jackson a famous 'A' celebrity American actor doing in a bar on the golden mile in Spain? … Well we had to find out… we approached him.

"Excuse me Sir…are you who we think you are"? I said…

He replied "Who do you think I am"

"Well… Samuel L Jackson"….we said

"Yes" he said.

Wow…. So we had a little chat with him asking what he was up to etc etc.

We didn't want to take up too much of his time as he was with a friend.

That was great I thought. I can't wait to tell everyone. Over the next few months I would tell everyone. Most found it strange but hey…. so a few months had passed. There was a Free Magazine that came out once a month about Marbella life. I picked up a copy and was flicking through. There was a 2 page article about an American guy called 'Wayne'.

I saw his photo… that wasn't Wayne that was Samuel L Jackson' I read on and it soon came to light that the guy that I thought was Jackson was actually an American guy called 'Wayne'. He was just chilling out in Spain for a few months. He would get asked all the time wherever he went 'Are you Samuel L Jackson' so he decided to create the fantasy that he was in so pleasing the admirers.

I couldn't believe it, I spent the last 3 months believing I had met Jackson, one of the greatest actors of all time instead I met 'Wayne'!! Lol

Yacht Party

Now Puerto Banus was certainly the land of the rich. This was most notable by some of the mega yachts…. I'm talking about boats that were worth hundreds of millions of pounds.

Through a couple of my Russian contacts and Alexander Dembinski, I got invited to a party on one of the mega yachts… yes please wouldn't mind a bit if that…. There were only about 30 people on the boat and 20 were seriously sexy scantily dressed women. I was buzzing but cautious… getting invited onto a mega boat by Russians can have its fear factor… I really didn't know what to expect…I knew I had to be on good behaviour ….. Which basically meant don't get pissed too quickly lol!! Oh well here goes… we were greeted onto the boat with a glass of champagne by what I would call a supermodel…on we went, "hello how are you"… 'hello how are you'… general chit chat… I told whoever asked what my profession was but I felt reluctant to ask the other guys too many questions about them. Maybe I didn't want to know or it was best if I didn't know anyway!! . We sat down for some light food. We we're served by women mostly in bikinis… most of the chit chat was amongst the Russians so I didn't have a clue what they were talking about.

Fine by me I was just eyeing up all the girls…you only saw things like this on films! How the fuck did some delusional cockney boy end up on a boat like this.

It was a couple of years later I learned the reason why I was probably invited on the boat which was I was being 'buttoned up' by Alexander Dembinski.

Anyway I was shown around the boat… there must have been a million pounds worth of gold fixtures and fittings… incredible.

At the back of the boat there was a small plunge pool … a couple of the girls were in there…we starting chatting… one of them took her bra off… fucking hell it was hot and during the day … I was wearing shorts…my chap couldn't contain himself and up it starts going. I'm trying to disguise it with my arm spread across the front of my shorts…what the fuck do I do…. So this chat is going on for a while and I was embarrassed to move anyway as I didn't want to see what was happening with my cock…then Alexander calls me …"Spyro… it's time to go now"…oh ok! I manoeuvred away from the girls and think I pulled it off … it went down very quickly after that….. However I was gutted… I must have only been on the boat an hour or so.

I sniffed a line of coke in the toilet while I was visualising snorting it from the nipples of the topless girl and was gearing myself up to shag one of the birds on the boat. For whatever reason I thought that that would be the end process…oh well…. But still gutted…I got off the boat and said bye to Alexander as we were going in different directions…I walked around like a peacock with its wings spread out… I was mixing it with the proper big boys. I was living the Fucking Dream. I couldn't wait to tell the boys at Linekers bar lol..

Our 'Deal' Theme Tune

2 of the mates I had in Marbella were Jeroen from Holland (I think I spelt his name right and Henrik from Norway… ultimately they ended up working for me. On our way out on a night out we started a chant. This chant was like a war cry for the perceived action…….well female action we were hoping to get that night. I don't know how it started or why really we chose that chant.

Now there's no word's to the chant other than the word 'La'. The word 'La' was sung to the tune of 'The animals came in three by three hurrah, hurrah'… in reference to Noah's Ark.

So what you need to do is sing that tune but just using the word 'La' where the tune speeds up and slows down you do the same.

So in effect the whole tune was:

"La La La La La ... La La La La.. La La... La La"... etc etc.

It was fucking hilarious. We used to sit in a taxi on the way to the port and then one of us would start it off...slowing slapping our hand against the chair and the dash board... it would get faster and louder... the taxi driver would think we were nuts but it always made us laugh.

Now this tune was also now being used as a celebration theme if someone in our office done a big deal. Maybe a £30,000 to £50,000 deal... it would usually be me.

The phone would go down after the deal and we would be off... all hands in the office would start the La La. La La etc slapping the desks in precise speed and ferocity with one hand and the other hand slapping our chested in equal rhythm... there could be 10 of us in our office.. The office was actually a shop front with large clear large glass fronting it. It could get quite loud in their once we started our celebration anthem... I think people that walked past must have thought we were nuts lol!

Navy Bar

The Navy bar on the second line in Puerto Banus was the favourite place for the evening's entertainment for holidaying golf groups. The Navy bar would be packed with brasses (prostitutes) every night waiting for their clients to attend. There would be at least 50 brasses in there. Mostly Brazilian, scantily dressed ready for business. Take your pick!

Prince Harry

I believe it was a Saturday lunchtime and from what I remember 'J' was with me at the time. We arrived at a famous Italian restaurant called De Bruno's. This was half way down the Golden Mile in Marbella. We sat outside and next to us was a lady who was by herself enjoying her lunch. The 3 of us got chatting and it turns out that she was the secretary or ex secretary of James Hewitt. You will remember I'm sure as it was well publicised that Princess Diana had apparently at some stage had an affair with Mr Hewitt. The secretary confirmed that this was true but not only that. She consorted that she knew that Prince Harry was the biological son of James Hewitt.

Ferrari Parade

Ferraris- most nights in the summer in Puerto Banus is the Ferrari circuit of the port… it's just a thing that's done where luxury cars like Ferraris drive a circuit around the port- quite pointless actually and a little vulgar…who are the dickheads that drive around the port showing off their apparent wealth. Puerto Banus is a den of evil in so many ways.

Meeting 'J' in 2008

I met 'J' in September 2008. Unfortunately this was the when the first signs of the problems in the business and my mental state was getting worse. We started to live together almost as soon as we met. Although things were going OK I started drinking more and more and 'J' was obviously becoming sick of it.

Soon after I met 'J', i rented a lovely villa in the mountains overlooking Marbella a few miles away. The villa was situated above a large lake. The views were spectacular. The villa was on 3 floors that led to a garden area with an infinity pool.

On a typical Saturday we would go to the Spa in the morning, followed by lunch and then off to Linekers to watch the football. It was the perfect day for me. However where after that I should have been happy after a nice day to go home and chill out with the girlfriend, I wanted more and more. Sometimes I would go back home with 'J' and then a couple of hours later go out again. It was an irresistible need to go out and drink alcohol and take cocaine. We would argue time and time again about me doing this but I literally could not stop myself.

'J' would be distraught and often leave and go and spend a couple of days around her friend's house. My behaviour was disgraceful and I am so sorry that 'J' had to endure the relentless addictive needs that I was going through at the time.

On Death Door Once again

One time I came back at ridiculous o'clock in the morning. Jenny was not there. I was on deaths door. I had literally overdosed on alcohol and cocaine. My heart must have been racing at 300 beats per minute. I was in pieces. There were tears flowing out from my eyes. I walked into the villa very slowly. I was scared that any sudden movements would send my heart over the edge and I would then collapse from a heart attack. That day I lay on the bed for hours waiting for my heart to stop. I was sure I was going to die. My heart rate would not slow. Would I ever see my children again I thought.

This happened on a few occasions. Can you imagine how fucked up I was to do this again after what happened this first time. I would spend the next day calling Jenny. I would beg her to come back. Again and again she did. However eventually it just got too much for her.

Mental Imbalance

Around 2009 to 2010 I felt significant changes in my brain. It was like there was a major chemical unbalance. My mood would alter very quickly. I became snappy, inpatient and irritable. One minute I was depressed and negative about my life the next I wanted to live until I was 100 years old.

This chemical unbalance was further exampled one time at Linekers bar. Spurs were playing that day. It was an early kick off so the bar was quite empty. I was with 'J', my mate Jack and his Mrs. So we settled down in front of the TV to watch the game. Soon after, a group of lads came into the bar. I believe they must have been on a stag holiday. It appeared that they were all Arsenal supporters. They were already quite drunk. They were singing Arsenal songs and anti-Tottenham songs. I thought nothing of it. I was with my girlfriend… However, a little while later, my brain just suddenly switched. I got angry. I stood up and told them to shut the fuck up.

An argument started and around 3 or 4 of them approached the slightly raised seated area that we were on. Then it went off. One of the guys threw a stool at us just missing my girlfriend. Another threw a glass… smash… just missed me and hit the back wall. I picked up a stool and was trying to beat them with it… it didn't last long as the bar men broke it up. We left. The guys I was with were shocked and scared. What the fuck was I doing. I was losing my fucking mind.

Cyprus 2010

On that visit to Cyprus with 'J' in 2010 we went to visit my auntie that had a small house in a village in the Troodos Mountain's. It's great up there. It's almost like you are in another world. It was so peaceful and secluded. So my auntie had a visitor that day. She was an old friend. I had met her on a couple of occasions in the past. To 'J's delight this person also happen to be the auntie of Pop star and TV celeb Peter Andre. 'J' was a big fan of his so was enthralled to meet one of his relatives. It was funny though as 'J' was acting like she had just met royalty.

My delusions of Grandeur were becoming quite extreme by this stage. I started to feel like it was my destiny to achieve something profound in the world with regards to getting rid of poverty and looking after orphaned children. This was evidenced by something I did whilst on this holiday in Cyprus. You will read more about this later on.

Back to Marbella - Russian Roulette 2010

It was another party night in Marbella… the syndicate of people I had been out that night was quite explosive… there was a mix of a few UK gangsters, a Dutch gangster and a few Russian gangsters… obviously I did not know the ins and outs of why all parties had come together. However, clearly it was some kind of business meeting but I had a feeling it was as much to do with guns as drugs on this occasion. It is a rarity for different gangs of gangsters to mix… usually too dangerous or there simply isn't any reason to do so. If gangsters have a beef they are more likely to employ a hit man to get at the other group rather than sit down between themselves and sort it out.

So it was an unusual event but must have been important. Although I mixed with one or two of the UK firms I never used to ask questions I was more interested in the debauchery that the evening was going to offer.

I had a good night, behaved myself and didn't do anything stupid as I was prone to doing on occasion.

There was an after party!! Ok great…. The after party involved about 10 of us which included the various gangster groups, a music producer/ top renowned DJ and some other guy. A crowd of such people that are going to a Party meant only one kind of party…..

Now Marbella has a lot of brothels, but some of them are quite spectacular. Grandiose buildings with indoor swimming pools and expensive wine menus… and not coincidentally we entered into one of them. We spread ourselves around on the comfortable sofas in a very large banqueting or chill out area… there were water springs, massive fish tanks and a swimming pool. There also of course many brasses floating about. At least 20 I would say… They were wearing bikinis, well at least the bottom halves of the bikinis anyway! The host came up to the 2 main guys in our group. The guys through wads of cash on the table - must have been at least £10,000 and soon the drinks started flowing. A bag of cocaine was thrown on the table and emptied into a couple of bowls. I am literally talking about a kg of cocaine…. Fuck me… this was paradise… or so I thought back then.

So the cocaine was poured from plastic bags into bowls. The owner then threw a packet of fresh uncut playing cards onto the table. One of the guys took a few cards and dug them into the pots of cocaine so the top halves of each card were sticking out. The playing cards were to be our snorting devices… makes a change from using a £10 note I thought!

Everyone was getting on it… the girls were flirting with us… one of the guys stripped to his underpants and jumped into the pool with 2 of the girls…this was going on for hours… guys… going in and out of rooms with different girls… 10 minute snort and drink and then back in again with another girl. I of course joined in. I knew no other way especially as I was addicted to everything by then, women, cocaine and alcohol.

So the party must have been going for a few hours and a couple of the 'G's got their guns out. Not in aggression but just comparing their straps etc. Now as I mentioned earlier there was this one guy in the group that I didn't really know much about… he wasn't one of the 'G's or like the DJ guy… he partied but was a lot more subdued than the rest of us. Anyway one of the 'G's shouted out … anyone for a game of Russian roulette? However, it did appear that the question was being posed to the odd guy out that I just explained. The odd guy laughed. I didn't though… I just grinned in anticipation. Now remember who we are dealing with… these people have no problems in killing other people but they must have been joking right!

So one of the Russian guys volunteers to go first…another guy spins the barrel … now I'm starting to get really worried… the DJ sitting next to me whispered don't worry there are no bullets in there… they are just playing around with the 'odd guy'

…. Thank fuck I thought… seriously I was shitting myself… the barrel stops spinning… straight into the mouth of one of the Russian G's, trigger pulled… nothing. Thank fuck for that but as I was told it was a fuck about by the DJ guy I was quite relaxed.

So the Russian guy says to the 'odd man' "why don't you have a go"?

The odd man was off his tits on alcohol and the white stuff… but I think he knew enough to believe that they were bluffing him and there wasn't really a bullet in the gun…the odd guy smiles and says… sure I will have a go… you only live once.

However soon after he starts fucking shitting himself… that's when the Russian guy came over with the gun. He showed him the empty barrel and showed him placing the bullet in …

At that point I started getting nervous again…the DJ looks over at me and says don't worry using his eyes and a bit of lip movement… 'This better be some kind of fucking trick' I thought!

The 'odd guy' sees the bullet going into the gun and his persona changes… he thought he was being tricked or bluffed as he believed there wasn't one actually in there. However, the odd fucker had just seen one being loaded!

His face colour changed to as white as snow… "You are not going to fucking bottle it are you"? said the Russian 'G'.

He said it with a threatening voice but this was part of the show as such. The odd guy didn't know what to do. He looked over at us… I was speechless then the DJ guy starts egging him on "come on are you a man or a pussy" he said

Sitting back from us the other 'G's were cheering him on… "Come on put the fucking gun in your mouth and show us how big your balls are"…the barrel was spun… I didn't think he would do it… the odd fucker put the gun in his mouth. The nutter pulled the fucking trigger.

Everyone started cheering. He got a few slaps on his back for his success. The odd man suddenly went from the quiet one, to the beast of the party. He jumped into the pool fully clothed and was jumping around like he had just won the fucking lottery.

He was obviously rejoicing in relief and proudness of his apparent manly strength and bottle in having the bollocks to undergo such a challenge.

He was allowed to celebrate for a good 20 minutes I would say before his celebrations were cut short. The Russian guy goes over to him again winds him up a bit then shows him it was a trick. I didn't get whether the bullet was in the barrel or not or it was set up on a lock where the bullet couldn't fall to the positioning of where it could be shot.

I was fucking relieved anyway…everyone started pissing themselves laughing…the odd guy didn't know whether to laugh or cry. So instead he just got up, snorted a big fat line and jumped back in the pool…What a fucking crazy. crazy night

The work of the evil

Mixing with gangsters was like floating with the devil. You never knew what could happen. There would always be a dangerous situation around the corner. I was to an extent putting my life into threat. It had taken me a while to realise this even though I was a little crazy myself at the time.

After the events of Russian Roulette that was me done. I couldn't put myself in a situation like that again. I am not a gangster nor did I want to be. What the fuck was I doing? I had children at home. Many people think it's cool being a 'G'…. I don't know about that but I can tell you it's dangerous and scary. I can advise people that forget what you see in films… it's not cool or clever. If you were in the middle of it all you would soon change your mind… Trust me…. Not unless you have a screw loose!

Spanish and Cyprus boutique hotel to stage world changing events

My delusions and grandiose thoughts were excelling. I wanted to create a small boutique hotel where world leader's would come and meet with me to discuss the world's problems such as poverty, hunger, religions and territories etc. The first place in scouted as being the appropriate place for such a meeting place, was on the borders of Puerto Banus and Nueva Andalusia.

Then I had a thought on a country within a country. This is where I revert back to the earlier Chapter of Cyprus 2010. Whilst in Cyprus with 'J' I put a £50,000 deposit down on a £1M villa. The villa was to be the central hub of a new country within the country of Cyprus, where people from all over the world would live. I decided that owning a villa there could be my base for when I started plans for the new country.

My thought process was that a square mile piece of land in Cyprus should be made into a world centre. In that I mean this area should somewhat represent all countries and religions of the world. It would be a peaceful neutral zone that no Country can invade. etc.

Within this area of land there would be buildings and areas that represent all countries of the word and have the religious buildings of the world… churches…synagogues, mosques, Indian and Chinese temples etc. On this land people will live that have come from all parts of the world and they will bring their children up there. It will be like a country within a country. However this country's purpose and direction is not one of capitalism or communism for example but is to learn about each other's races and religions and to create a peaceful community that slowly and over the years show the rest of the world what life should really be all about. There would be no poverty. Everyone would live equally as brothers and sisters and love as to the instruction of God

The fact that we are 'apparently' so far the only known intelligent species in the universe yet we fight each other over religion and territory is scandalous, ludicrous.

Delusional or Real

I know that your initial thoughts maybe that I am insane or delusional. I guess you have every right to think that as the traits that I am expressing are clearly ones of a Bi Polar sufferer that also suffers with Psychosis which I have been diagnosed as having However in the next few pages you will be evidenced with something that happened and was evidenced that will blow your mind.

Problems with Alexander Dembinski

So you will have read earlier that Alexander owed me a considerable amount of wine stock. Around 2 years later it was time to start delivering stock from the also great 2006 vintage.

It was 2009 now. Alexander had admitted that he had been let down or even scammed with the stock from the 2005 vintage. Although he had given me some cash back ... by now less than £100,000 there was still a-lot of stock from that vintage still owing. Alexander said that he was not able to get any stock from the 2005 vintage. So we agreed that he would convert what he owed me in 2005 stock on to 2006 stock. However, due to the losses he claimed that he had also been subjected to that the stock instead of being delivered in 2009 would be delivered in 2010.

One of the unfortunate consequences of being a bi polar sufferer is that you can be very gullible. I suppose most normal minded people at this stage would have thought that I was being conned… mugged off.

It is only later I realised that in reality the chances were that I had been scammed. I had been 'led down the garden path' by Dembinski. I don't know if it was a complete con by Dembinski or partly where he had lost money too by being defrauded.

This cycle of events carried on until 2011. I would continue to receive some cash back but with false promises. By now I was owed millions of pounds of stock. The companies were fucked but I still in my delusional bi polar mind believed that somehow everything would come good.

I felt that I had to keep fighting for the business. I was sure that Alexander would send me the stock eventually or worst case scenario that my investments in Proventus Renewables would come to fruition and bail me out if there was a problem. This is why I kept the business going. I was taking financial risks but once again I thought that this was the right thing to do as in fact this was a normal process in my mind. Unfortunately once again, one of the traits of Bi Polar disorder is unknowingly taking financial risks.

Proventus Renewables - Scammed Again?

Around 2008 I was introduced to an Indian businessman from Bedford. He was the owner of an investment company. He was also a major shareholder in two new business ventures. These were called Symbiosis and Proventus Renewables. Symbiosis was a medical company and Proventus Renewables was a wind farm energy company. I met with this guy on a couple of occasions and once again I was convinced that what he was offering was a sure fire winner. I was especially impressed with the Proventus project. I noticed some good newspaper articles about the project in the Irish times. One of his partners was a reasonably well known businessman, come politician. It all added up and seemed credible. I was persuaded that the companies would end up being worth hundreds of millions of pounds.

Therefore an investment then could have supplied me with a massive windfall.

Over the next couple of years I invested hundreds of thousands of pounds into the project. I was using what I deemed to be profits from the wine company to purchase stock in the 2 projects.

My feeling then was that if for some reason Alexander Dembinski continued to fail in providing me with the wine stock,

I would have this covered by the anticipated enormous profits I would make in these 2 other projects.

In my delusional and gullible mind one way or another, money was going to be made and everything would turn out to be just fine.

This is the reason I continued trading in 2011 and 2012. I still somehow and incredibly believed that Alexander would come good on delivery of the wine stock, but in any case I was about to make tens of millions of pounds on the other projects......or so I believed.

So I convinced myself that the wine business was not insolvent and continued trading.

I waited and waited for the 2 new projects to come to fruition but nothing happened. It appears once again I was led down the garden path by others and my delusional bi polar mind could not work out that once again this was happening.

The Indian chap that introduced these 2 new projects was convicted and sent to jail for fraudulent activities in one of the companies and the other company was shut down in 2017.

On another Level

All of my addictions were in full flight by around 2010.. Alcohol... smoking... cocaine.... and women.

500 Shades of Sex!!

I'm not going to lie but if I didn't pull a girl on a night out I often hooked up with a brass (prostitute). These ladies would frequent many of the 'normal' bars that tourists did. You couldn't get away from them… surrounded by them… mainly Brazilians.

Try sticking £100 or £200 in your mates pocket at the end of a night and say to him there's 10 sexy Brazilians over there go and pick one. Most blokes I know would be straight over there without a second thought.

Now imagine me - that always had access to hundreds of pounds at the end of the night and these girls are standing in front of you. I had the money… I didn't want the party to end.

What's more unfortunate is that by being a Bi Polar sufferer you are even more inclined to continuing seeking pleasurable activities. Especially as I already would have been very merry or high due to my alcohol and cocaine intake.

I couldn't help it… I had to get a brass…unfortunately this kind of debauchery continued over much of my time whilst living in Marbella…. I literally couldn't stop myself… an addiction that had to be satisfied…but it got worse.

Now for me having a mix of alcohol, cocaine and Viagra… it meant I could have a 'stiffy' and therefore sex for hours without ejaculating. Not that my meetings were all about the sex.

It was the on-going party. My addictions were now getting out of control. Having one woman at a time wasn't enough…2 then 3 then 4….. It was now becoming orgies… me and a multiple of other women…I was losing the plot…

Women loving women

My sexual addiction had upgraded itself to higher levels of needs. It wasn't enough anymore to have sex with one or two brasses. I needed something else. It was time for lesbian orgies.

I had been with 2 girls on loads of occasions where there was lesbian sex. I suppose like most blokes I really enjoyed it.

I wanted to take things up another level. So I organised a lesbian orgy involving 3 women this time.

The women were all working escorts and I had met all 3 of them before.

On a usual night out, I was standing by the bar. This was one of those bars where 80% of its clients were escorts.

I called one girl over and started discussing my plan. She then picked out another 2 girls that would join the party.

The four of us spent some time having a few drinks and a dance.

I believe that all 3 girls were Brazilian. Two of the girls I would say were in their early to mid-thirties and loved lesbian sex and was something they were well up for. The third lady was a little younger, maybe in her mid to late 20s. She professed that she had often thought about sex with another girl but had never actually done it before.

She seemed especially excited at the prospect of what was to come that evening.

It was soon after we left the bar. We didn't have far to walk to reach our nest for the evening.

I bought a couple of bottles of wine with us and we were all packing cocaine.

We had a sip of wine and a big line. The girls started to undress. It appears that the 2 older girls were going to give the younger 'lesbian virgin' a night to remember.

They removed all of her clothing. They were gently stroking her hair and her breasts. One of the older girls starts licking, kissing and sucking the younger girl's breasts. The other is kissing her passionately on the lips.

Her whole body was now being kissed. The younger girl was shaking in anticipation of ecstasy.

The hand of one of the experienced girl's, moves towards the younger girl's vagina. Very softly she stroked the outside. I could see that her pussy was already starting to get wet.

With the finger movements continuing, they slowly with each stroke enter the girls vagina… and with ever stroke entering deeper and deeper inside her.

I by now have a proper hard on. I'm letting the girls do what they wanted and I would have a part to play here and there but with most of the focus being left to the 3 girls to carry out.

Whilst her pussy is becoming wetter and wetter the other girl joins in down below. So one of the girls is 'wanking' the girl off with her fingers and the other has now also joined in using her mouth.

Her mouth is taking long strides and moving up and down the whole pussy. Then there is more concentration as she licks the top of the cliterous at speed.

The younger girl is looking up at the ceiling. There is ecstasy in her eyes. She is clenching the bed sheets with both hands.

Her groans are becoming loader. She looks at me and then grabs my stiff cock. She tells me to put it in her mouth.

She is sucking me hard… really hard… the two other girls are doing what they are doing.

The girl is now screaming in ecstasy… I can see her vagina gushing out fluids and could feel her body orgasming.

We kept pounding away at her in our own ways. This went on for some time then there was the final release of ecstasy. She pushed her hands on the head and arm of the girls. She couldn't take it anymore…she signalled for them to stop. The girls moved away. There was a small puddle of fluid on the bed sheet by her vagina.

The girl had goosebumps, she was still shaking and breathing heavily.

She seemed overwhelmed, her face was blushed. 'Oh my, oh my' she proclaimed.

'That was unbelievable' she said.

That evening continued in that manor for a few hours.

It gave me the extra fix that satisfied my addiction.

This was on another level.

Angels of God - First Encounter - 2010

The first escort was already in the room but I was out of control I wanted more. They started coming in one by one. Then something amazing happened. The second one walked in.

I was blown away, shocked really fucking scared… the woman was 8ft tall… a perfectly shaped female body but very slim with a tight small waste… was this real?… I must have been dreaming or hallucinating… then another came in then another.

What the fuck was going on… had I been abducted by aliens? This wasn't really happening…. I sat on the bed motionless. The women or whatever they were circled the bed.

There were 2 normal skin coloured females but one was a light blue colour. They had soft and very slightly oily skin. There was no hair on their bodies anywhere. They were huge but slender at the same time. They had large eyes that all appeared to be a very light blue in colour.

I could hear music that seemed to be coming out from their bodies… it was the most tranquil and beautiful music I had ever heard. They then started moving their hands and arms in a soft and delicate way almost like they were dancing to the music or even orchestrating it.

I felt a tingling throughout my body that was the most sensational feeling I had ever had. The women would start placing their hands on the other women. One blew out a stream of beautifully coloured flowers from her mouth…. While another was blowing out a rainbow with a distinct colour that I don't believe I had ever seen before.

There were music notes also coming out… this was fucking incredible… what was happening… am I in heaven? It was as though everyone in the room was performing in acts of sexual pleasure yet there were none of the usual things happening that you would associate with sex. It was mind blowing…

The angels were singing to me in Greek. It was such a beautiful sound. The power of the moment was so exhilarating. I had never felt anything like this before. My mind fell deeper into the ambiance and trance of the moment and contained speeds of thought that no one can comprehend unless you experience it. I could see and feel everything in a musical way.

The 'normal' girl that had initially come into the room was sitting right next to me. Clearly she was experiencing the same thing. She was also speechless. She looked at me in ecstasy.

This continued for a while. I have no idea how long. It could have been an hour or a lot more.

These 'Angels' were sending me clear messages on a multitude of things. This included love, sex, honour, the after-life and helping those in need. The most prominent message they were in effect injecting into my mind was the Matrix of Universes.

A Complex Matrix – A Multi Universe Trance State of Mind

There very well may be nine levels of hell as written in Dante's Inferno but when I look at the matrix of life as was presented to me by the Angels on this particular night, then I believe there are for more levels overall – good and not so good.

The matrix of universal life expands so profoundly through intricacies of levels that there is a place for everyone in their next spiritual or embodied life. Although one's body will be different if they are given a body at all, the spirit remains the same.

The spirit will know had to better it's previous life and of course have been given Free Will by God to do so.

I believe it must have been around 1999 that I can first remember me having sleepless nights due to lengthy trance like states of mind where I would visualise spectacular things and scenarios.

That was the first time I believe that I was receiving messages about an incredible scene of complex matrices in never ending universes. There would be bright white lines 'Zig Zagging' and crossing over each other... thousands of them, never ending and going from one direction to another.

This was happening again but with the Angels present it was much more of an intense feeling of clarity.

I was trying to understand what I was seeing. It appeared that it was a message explaining the spiritual movements of beings crossing from one existence to another in a different part of the universe or crossing over to another universe altogether

It was like a library of patterns of movement that were sending a being from one life to the next. Where the being would end up would depend on what they had done in their previous life. I felt that some beings were going to greater places than others. Although it appeared that all places were at least ok just that some were better than others. There was no hell but it appears that those who had not lived a life that was in line with how God would have wanted could not be taken to a higher plane of living or being… almost like that had to start again from the beginning…this was an infinite matrix of ever-lasting life… beings would be somewhat similar to themselves from a previous life but not exactly…you can never be exactly you again. A matrix of different levels of potential happiness and intelligence depending on what you achieved in your previous life.

The Brazilian Messenger

The girl that was in the room with the 3 angels experienced what I experienced. After the experience I left hurriedly from the Madame's house. The girl/escort chased me. She was crying … 'what has just happened' she shouted at me. I didn't know. I jumped in a taxi and we sped off.

I saw the girl some days later sitting at a coffee shop during the day. I approached her. She had been profoundly overcome by what happened. 'So it was all real then' I proclaimed to myself within my thoughts.

We didn't really know what to say to each other. We knew by seeing each other that what happened was real. She said that she was going to leave Spain and go back to Brazil. She had 2 young children that were being looked after by her parents. She said she needed to be with them after the experience we had. She also explained that she had received similar messages that I had.

"Are we prophets" she said to me.

I didn't know how to answer that. We held hands and looked at each other direct in the eyes. We both cried again.

"We must do something" she said to me.

"I know" I said but I had no idea at the time.

"See you, I have to go, I'm flying to Brazil tomorrow morning" she said.

I gave her a cuddle and she left. I never saw her again.

Where are the Angels

The night with the Angels was 2 weeks ago now. I never went out again during that 2 week period. I was waiting for the Angels. I was praying that I would see them again. I could not take the wait anymore. I had to see them.

I decided to go to the Madame's house where I had encountered the Angels 2 weeks earlier.

I called in a girl/escort and waited. Nothing happened. I called in another and then another but none of these were the Angels.

A couple of hours later I left the 'Madame's' house. The sunlight was too much for my eyes.

I was mentally fucked and distressed that I had not seen the Angels.

Suddenly a huge cloud frazzled my brain and I felt horrendously depressed. I managed to flag a taxi down and got in. I literally held my head in my hands

The taxi driver asked what the matter was and I just saying that I had a very big problem but I didn't know what it actually was.

Living with HIV…for just 24 hours?

So in 2010 my doctors in Marbella wanted to do some yearly blood tests on me… ok… he asked if I would like to have a HIV test…although I had received blood test for HIV previously and was obviously fine… this time I felt a little nervy about it.

You will have read in the book my sexual exploits whilst living in Spain so I had increased my chances of getting HIV.

So I agreed to the test…. I told my girlfriend at the time …. You already know her as 'J'.

However she didn't seem to have any concerns about it. However it wasn't one of those tests where you could wait just an hour or two to get the results. As usual as I had received several tests before, it was a really scary time while you are waiting for the results.

Anyway my results were coming the next day.

I got a call from the surgery the next day… here we go…. The doctors said… "Mr Constantino we have detected a virus in your system and I'm sorry to say it appears that you have the HIV virus"…

My heart sank …. I couldn't believe it….he then said 'we are continuing to look at the blood sample so I would like you to come to the surgery later this afternoon'.

'Fuck me I've be got HIV' ...I spoke with 'J' but strangely enough she didn't panic or get stressed about it!

'J' and I went to the doctors that afternoon. The doctor said that they were still looking at the blood sample but were pretty sure that I had been infected with the HIV virus. He proceeded to say that he would contact me later that day or in the morning with a final confirmation.

'J' and I left the surgery and walked to the beach that was 5 minutes away. You can't ever imagine how I felt but also the worry I had that if I had it then I may have passed the virus onto 'J'. I presumed that if I had the virus it would have been caught through my dangerous past sexual exploits and not through 'J'.

Anyway we sat on the beach and discussed it. We all know the stigma that was related to having HIV and I didn't know how this would affect the rest of my/our lives.

However 'J' seemed to be extremely calm in the situation especially considering that if I had the Virus then so might she.

I believed I was in tears on the beach and asked if she was going to leave me and she said no.

So it comes to the next day and by then it had been close to 24 hours since we had been given the news. You can imagine what was going through my brain during that time. To get that kind of news almost feels like the end of the world...

The phone rang..."Mr Constantino... I have some good news for you".... 'Actually the virus that we thought was HIV is not... it is another kind of virus'.

'So I am pleased to say that you are Not HIV positive'!!

What the fuck! I couldn't believe it… this was one of the best feelings of my life… imagine Spurs scoring the winner in the Champions league final against Arsenal…. I was jumping with joy. I ran to 'J' and informed her. She was obviously very happy.

How the fuck could they have got something like that wrong - I didn't think that sort of mistake could happen nor could be allowed to happen?

My doctor's surgery was not some Mickey Mouse establishment. It was a private surgery … with well renowned Doctors and a very happy client base of patients.

It just seemed all a bit strange for me…. Especially as 'J' seemed to take the whole thing in her stride… I just have this feeling and suspicion about the whole thing…I will keep that to myself though!

Return of the Angels of God – Early 2011

It was a good few months now since I had seen the Angels and wondered if I ever would again. Jenny was out for the day. It wasn't an especially warm day as it was earlier in the year. I had a friend round and we were sitting by the outside table under the grape vines. My mate Jorgin went down to the next level to use the swimming pool. I was sitting there looking down at the view and seeing him having a swim.

I turned around and 'bang' there they were, the 3 Angels. They looked at me but this time there was a feeling of not only happiness in their eyes but sadness also. The Matrix lit up again but this time it was not just being shared in our minds but there it was appearing as a hologram in front of us.

I concentrated eagerly. I needed to know more. Why were they sending me these messages?

What if anything did I have to do? I believe they knew I was asking them the questions and what those questions were. My feeling or interpretation was that I would know when the time came.

Like a gust of wind the 3 Angels morphed into each other and sped off in a light ball into the sky.

I look over the balcony towards the light ball – Jorgin shouts out "what the fuck was that" he had seen the light ball shooting off. He came back upstairs.

"Did you see that mate…What the fuck was it" he said

I explained to him what had happened. I'm not sure if he believed me or not, but was sure he saw the ball of light. We talk about it every now and again. I know that what happened was real.

On the road to now where – Beach Battle

I was found 6 miles from where I lived by someone that happened to recognise me. It appeared I had walked 6 miles during that day. I must have been in a 'Manic' Bi polar episode.

There is no way I would have walked that far otherwise….. trust me that's for people that like exercise!

I had no idea why I was walking or where I was going. I just remember I had to keep moving keep walking. Something was telling me I had to walk and walk.

So a guy that I knew called Ben pulls up by me in his car – "Hello mate where are you off to"? Ben Says.

I must have clicked out of the manic episode "I'm not sure mate" I said.

"Are you ok Bruv" he says…..."Yeah I've just had an argument with 'J', I decided to tell him, so I decided to walk it off.

It was early evening and Ben was off to watch the football at a Bar 3 or 4 miles down the road. 'You coming' he said. I jumped in and thought 'football and beer' that sounds like a good plan.

So we arrived at this Bar. This was about 10 miles out of Marbella on a very small coastal town mainly inhabited by Spanish residents although there was a fair sized English ex pat community living there. I had been there a couple of times over the years. A very friendly, quiet and down to earth place which was very unlike Marbella!

Like most bars on the Costa del Sol this one was open late. The football had finished and it now turned into a small nightclub. I met a couple of others there that I knew from Puerto Banus and we carried on the evening.

It was getting late, I'm guessing about 3am. I was pissed but also knackered. The long walk from yesterday had got to me. I just wanted to go to sleep.

I got outside and was looking for taxis. There were none about. I asked someone and they said there are very few about as most people that visit this bar were locals and they could walk home.

The guys I knew at the bar had left earlier.

'Fuck what am I going to do' I thought.

I needed to sleep… I walked onto the beach and looked for a spot to crash out. I found a broken disused plastic sun bed.

I collapsed on it and must have fallen asleep….

I don't know how long I had been sleeping. My eyes opened when I heard what I thought was a gun shot. A blue light was flashing.

I looked along the beach to where there was a rock pier that was around 100 metres away. The rock pier curled round into a shape of the letter 'C' and was around 50 meters into the sea.

There was some shouting by the rocks. There were 2 boats. One was a police boat and that's where the blue flashing lights were coming from. The other boat was more like a fishing boat. Smaller in size and white in colour.

I sat up. It took me a few seconds to work out what was going on.

Bang, another sound of a Gun-shot.

The police boat was trapping the smaller boat against the rocks.

It was almost certainly a drug smuggling operation that had been caught out.

As mentioned earlier in my story, the Costa del Sol is a prime location for drug smuggling.

The drugs come via Gibraltar and Africa. They are just a few miles away from the coast of the Costa del Sol.

They then get distributed by drug gangs around Europe from Spain.

It was starting to get light. I could see 2 police officers in Sniper positions. They must have only been 100ft away from me.

This was too close for comfort. It was time for me to get the fuck out of there.

Before I could even stand up I heard....

'Stay down, stay down' first in Spanish and then in English.

'What the fuck' I thought.

I turned to the right and there was a fucking machine gun pointing at me.

'Don't move, put your hands behind your head'

One of the officers stands in front of me and the other to the side of me with his strap (gun) pointing at my head.

In Spanish the officer proceeds to say something like 'what are you doing here… are you holding a gun' ….my brain was still frazzled from the previous night's entertainment and having practically no sleep. I could barely speak.

I respond to the officer in a mix of English and Spanish…'I'm just sleeping… I was at the bar… I pointed to the bar some 50 yards behind me… I'm tired…. I had too much to drink.'

The officer's start talking to each other…I look over at the boats. The small boat which was obviously smuggling drugs or guns, appeared to have been swarmed by police.

It looked like they had it under control.

I sat there. The police officers said nothing for a few minutes. The gun was still pointing at my head.

'I'm fucked' I thought. They are thinking that I have something to do with the smuggling operation.

I was so tired. I could barely keep my eyes open.

By now I could maybe see a further 10 police officers paroling the beach out in front of me.

To my right a police van pulls over.

Police officers from the van start walking towards us.

"We found him here boss" (said the officer that had been questioning me a few minutes earlier) to the senior officer that just arrived.

The senior officer shouts "Stand up" to me. I stand up. He looks at me in the eyes. Then up and down like I was a piece of shit.

'I'm fucked now' I thought.

"What are you doing here" he says.

I repeated what I had said to the other officer earlier.

"There were no taxis to get home" I pleaded

I hear a shout from behind us in Spanish… "What's going on" a male voiced bellowed?

It turned out to be the owner or manager from the bar. I wasn't quite sure which he was.

The Senior Officer and the Bar manager start talking. The bar manager recognised me from a few hours earlier as being at the bar.

"He was drinking all night" the manager said to the officer.

The officer looked me in the eyes again and realised I was in a state due to alcohol and tiredness and probably realised that I was just a piss head that didn't make it home rather than an organised gangster that was part of a drug smuggling operation. lol!

The senior officer asked me where I lived. I told him.

He gave me a little slap to the face and said "Fuck off. Go home. Don't come back here"

I couldn't believe it. They were letting me go.

I put my arms down from behind my head. I walked backwards a few steps. I staggered past the bar then up a small hill that took me back onto the main road.

I must have walked a mile on the main road. I waited and waited for a taxi to pass me. Soon I managed to flag one down.

I felt like I had just been in an episode of a gangster film. It was surreal.

I never told anyone what happened as I was scared that the leaders of the smuggling operation would somehow find out that I was on the beach for the failed operation and that I had either something to do with its failure or that I might have information that could assist them. Either way it didn't matter, it's just not something I felt safe in publicising at the time.

Leaving Spain – Back to England

After the events on the beach a couple of weeks earlier, I knew my time was up in Spain. I had to get out or I am sure I would somehow have ended up dying.

The company owed millions of pounds. Spain had ruined me. I was getting heavier, and I was drinking and snorting even more than usual. Some months earlier I had discussed moving back to England with 'J' and this would happen sooner or later but not together.

In August 2011 Jenny finally left me for good. The turmoil's of the previous 3 years had become too much. It actually happened in Croatia at my Godbrother's wedding. The night before the wedding we were all out having a meal. On the way back to the hotel I got into an argument with 'J'. To be honest I think it had got to a stage that I repulsed her due to my carrying's on. I don't blame the girl. She packed her bag that night, moved to another room in the hotel and by the time I got up the next morning she had already left to go back to the UK.

We both had to spend some weeks back in Spain sorting our things out for the move back to England and we actually ended up staying with each other for 6 weeks, but not as a couple.

I saw 'J' one more time after that in October 2011

However I would not move back to England unless my ex-wife and kids also moved back.

I spoke with Ann. She could see that I was having many problems. Ann and the kids were quite happy in Spain but were also ok with moving back to England.

Ok so it was now or never. I moved back in August 2011. I sorted out a new school for the girls and somewhere for them to live. They moved back in January 2012.

Calling Tim in the middle of the night with grandiose plans – 2011-2012

So I was back in England now. My mate Tim would experience on occasion my manic episodes of Bi Polar and I think it may have been him that first suggested that I had some kind of psychosis.

This would often be demonstrated when I would call him in the middle of the night when he would be sleeping. I would spurt out grandiose ideas and plans and complex schemes of how I was going to make £100m in that forthcoming year. It all made sense to me but eventually started pissing Tim off.

I don't really know for sure what he thought was going through my mind or if I was crazy.

Being Bi Polar – Diagnosis October 2012

In May 2012 I started dating Mel. Good looking girl from Kent. I had only been back from living in Spain for about 9 months. I was living in Buckhurst Hill at the time and still working the wine business.

She was a medical secretary so had some good knowledge of medical conditions. After only a few months of dating she was getting concerned about my mental health due to strange behaviour and suggested to me I should see a psychiatrist as she thought I was suffering with Bi Polar Disorder.

I still had no idea at the time what Bi Polar Disorder was. I didn't really want to see a psychiatrist but Mel insisted. So in October 2012 an appointment was made to see a psychiatrist at Basildon Mental Health Unit. After a few hours of investigations by a psychological nurse and then 2 psychiatrists and assistance from Mel as to what she had been witnessing, I was diagnosed with Bi Polar Disorder including Psychosis and Alcohol Related problems

What is Bi Polar Disorder

People with bipolar experience both episodes of severe depression and episodes of mania – overwhelming joy, excitement or happiness, huge energy, a reduced need for sleep, and reduced inhibitions.

Depression

During a period of depression, your symptoms may include:

- **Feeling sad, hopeless or irritable most of the time**
- **Lacking energy**
- **Difficulty concentrating and remembering things**
- **Loss of interest in everyday activities**
- **Feelings of emptiness or worthlessness**
- **Feelings of guilt and despair**

- Feeling pessimistic about everything
- Self-doubt
- Being delusional, having hallucinations and disturbed or illogical thinking
- Suicidal thoughts
- Mania

The manic phase of bipolar disorder may include:

- Feeling very happy, elated or overjoyed
- Talking very quickly
- Feeling full of energy
- Feeling self-important
- Feeling full of great new ideas and having important plans
- Being easily distracted
- Being easily irritated or agitated
- Being delusional, having hallucinations and disturbed or illogical thinking
- Doing things that often have disastrous consequences – such as spending large sums of money on expensive and sometimes unaffordable items
- Making decisions or saying things that are out of character and that others see as being risky or harmful
- Taking Financial Risks
- Being led down the Garden path by others

- **Grandiose Ideas**

- **Getting Involved in Complex Investment Schemes**

It is well documented that it is believed that many sufferers of bi polar disorder have very creative minds and can reach a higher intelligence. My self-examination would suggest that this could very well be so. Did you know that Einstein suffered with Bi-Polar. It is argued that this condition at least partially made him the extraordinary mathematician he was. He could see mathematical equations that no one else could and still can't to a certain extent.

Maybe this skill or genius was passed onto him by superior beings. In effect he was a prophet of mathematics.

I am no Einstein but I do know that I on occasion receive as you will have read receive messages from a more superior or powerful force and I have tried to express those messages where I can within this book.

I therefore kindly request to all those other sufferers of Bi Polar that if you believe that you understand something to a higher level than most then this is for a reason and therefore you must be open with your thoughts and not hide away for a fear of being ridiculed as crazy.

There is something to learn from each of us.

After the consultation at Basildon Mental Health Unit I was instructed to crate daily mood diaries for the next 6 months. I then returned to see the psychiatrists. They, on the basis of my mood diaries increased my dosage of medication that treats manic episodes.

I started to study the illness. This is when it became clear as to why I often acted so strangely, my addictions and my delusions etc. It was a very scary period for me. Was I mad? Did I live in a different psychological World? Had my business failings been down to my mental illness? Was I going to die?

Mel stuck with me and we were supposed to have an engagement party that Christmas in 2012 in Billericay. However I took the news badly from the psychiatrists and found myself drinking even more alcohol and arguing with Mel. We had to call the engagement party off as I wasn't in any fit state to be with anyone but Mel stuck by me.

Arrested

It was early February 2013. Mel and I were asleep in our bedroom in a house that I had rented in Cray's Hill in the Billericay area. It was 7am. There was a knock on the door. I got up and looked out of the window. There were 2 police officers outside with 2 normally dressed persons.

I went downstairs, opened the door. "Mr Constantinos" they said.

"Yes" I said.

"You are under arrest for the allegations of fraud that have been made against you in relation to wine Investment activities"

I said nothing. I showed them where all of my business files and lap top were. The police officers then took me to Basildon Police Station. I was booked in and then some hours later, 2 officers from Trading Standards were present with 2 police officers for questioning.

My records had shown that I had turned over £10 Million in wine sales around a 5 to 6 year period

I was later released and placed on bail.

My Legal Defence Team

By November 2013 I had secured a Legal Defence team that were to represent me before and during trial. I initially met with the solicitors which seemed fine and they informed me of the 'highly rated QC' that would be representing me. This was the beginning of the catastrophe as far as I was concerned.

I informed the solicitor that I was Bi Polar sufferer that included Psychosis. The solicitor agreed with the QC that Bi Polar was to be the basis of my defence. So it should have been. You will have read earlier that the traits and characteristics of Bi Polar Disorder have a complete nexus with how the businesses were run.

I provided the solicitor with large amounts of Medical evidence for the disorder.

Indeed this was once again supported when the solicitors wrote to my GP who confirmed the documents etc. There was sufficient evidence to suggest that had I received a Fair Trial that the judge and more importantly the Jury may have found me not guilty due to the extreme debilitating effects that the Bi Polar was having on my mind, health and overall life.

Incredibly, just 2 to 3 months before trial, having had my medical evidence for well over a year that categorically and clearly had confirmed diagnosis of Bi Polar disorder and that I was on medication for it, the solicitor said that they had an issue with the documents and wanted second opinions. 'What is the problem' I said. 'Oh its nothing too important …you don't have to worry about it the solicitor said.

So for some unknown reason the solicitors instructed me to go and see a private psychiatrist somewhere in Southend. I visited the psychiatrist for an hour. In a later report this psychiatrist stated that:

- **I had indeed been diagnosed by Basildon Mental Health Unit as being a Bi Polar sufferer.**

- **I was on medication for the disorder**

- **However, he was not an expert in Bi Polar Disorder**

- **He was not provided with all of my medical notes**

- **That he would need to see me at least 2 or 3 times before diagnosing or excluding a diagnosis of Bi Polar Disorder**

- **That he would have preferred it that someone else had attended the consultation with me to discuss witnessed manic episodes as many suffers of manic episodes don't actually remember what happened.**

- **Therefore on the basis of all of the above his report would have to be Preliminary and therefore could not confirm for sure in his opinion after one consultation whether I was Bi polar or not**

So why did the Solicitor/Trial Defence Counsel seek a further report to the original one provided by Basildon Metal Health Unit when it was not needed? Well it turns out that they made a shocking error so bad in their review of my original documents that this would lead them to not only act negligently, but in my opinion criminally and with perjury which I can absolutely prove as it is well documented.

Basically the Solicitor saw a '?' Next to the diagnosis of Bi Polar Disorder thinking that it was questioning whether I had Bi polar Disorder. However anyone could see from the document that it wasn't questioning whether I had Bi Polar Disorder at all. It was questioning whether Bi Polar or Alcohol was the Primary or secondary problem meaning that both conditions existed. Indeed not only that, further within the medical documents it clearly states that I was put on a medication that was for Bi Polar and Psychosis.

The Solicitors also had documents from my revisit to the psychiatrist at Basildon Mental Health Unit in April 2013 that confirmed and increased the dosage of the medication and that my further weight gain could very well have been due to The 'Bi Polar Medication' that I was on.

So after the psychiatrist that they hired in Southend confirmed that I indeed had been diagnosed by Basildon Mental Health Unit as being a Bi Polar sufferer the Solicitor should have realised his mistake and produced that medical information to the court at trial.

However and instead what happened next appears to be an act of criminality on their part. It is evident that they wanted to sabotage my Bi Polar defence and sacrifice me in order to save themselves looking stupid in court and therefore undermining their abilities as professionals.

They made me see another psychologist who confirmed that I had severe alcohol problems and was at risk of suicide but she was lacking a lot of medical information for her to make an accurate diagnosis. This was similar as to what the psychiatrist from Southend had said.

What the fuck were the solicitors up to? They were making a mess of everything. Not only that but they arranged an appointment with a neurologist who ultimately that feared brain damage due to either the accident or severe alcohol abuse and wanted me to have another test. The solicitors failed to arrange this second test.

To summarise, they already had clear and comprehensive reports from Basildon Mental Health Unit spanning 6 months and with 2 different psychiatrists at the material time of the alleged offending that I was a Bi polar sufferer.

They had reports that by the time of the Trial I had been on medication for Bi Polar for more than 2.5 years

They also had a report from a psychologist that I had severe problems with alcohol and that I was at high risk of suicide

They also had a request from a neurologist for further examinations for my brain as he feared brain damage which the solicitors failed to arrange.

However due to their negligence in the first place, had they provided the court with all of the medical information they would have looked extremely unprofessional. As stated above they sacrificed me in order to save themselves. Remember this was a big case so such negligence on the part of my legal defence team could have ruined them.

Instead they forced me to somehow believe that I did not have Bi polar disorder and brushed away the alcohol, suicide and brain damage issues.

I went to trial without the Judge or Jury knowing any of this information at all. I was helpless. I didn't know what to do. They fucked me over.

You will note through the course of this book my on-going battle for justice for my case. In late 2023 or early 2024 I will be publishing a new book that I believe will be entitled.

'Corruption within The UK Justice System'.

This book will provide all of the documents that relate to my case before, during and after trial. I will talk more about this later on

The Old Bailey

My trial for allegations of fraud started in early June 2015.

I had the same journey every day for those 4 weeks to the Old Bailey for my trial. I was staying at my cousins very small studio flat in Earl's Court … sleeping on the floor most of the time but it took less than half an hour to get to the Old Bailey.

Pretty much every previous night I had been drinking alcohol and sniffing cocaine. So I was often a little worse for wear whilst sitting in the dock for a few hours every day. I just wanted each day to be over with.

So the trial had only started literally 2 days earlier. I was walking around Earl's Court and my mate was driving passed. We clocked each other and he pulled over down the road.

"Mate" he said… "Have you seen the newspapers and internet"?

"Why what's up" I said.

"You are on the front page of the Mail online".

This was obviously to do with my case.

We had a quick chat and then I moved on to go and check out what was being said. Although I was only 2 days into trial the

Mail online had already found me guilty! There was a picture of me which was the worst picture ever taken of me. I looked fucking awful and there was a description of what I had apparently done along with details of how I allegedly spent the money. Holidays to New York and Miami, private schools and expensive watches!

Every morning when arriving at St Paul's Cathedral tube station which is a 5 minute walk from the Old Bailey, I was weary of the Paparazzi. I had spotted them from day one. When I saw them I would cover my face with my bag but unknowingly the fuckers got me full on one day. They had the photo and then made the assumed headline.

Later that day I was getting calls from all over… "Did you know you are front page news"…

"Yes I fucking know" …… not good

On one occasion in the dock at the old Bailey it felt very surreal …. I wasn't actually sure if I was there or not.

I must have been hallucinating towards the end of the trial as often when I looked over at the head juror I would see the face of what seemed the devil shinning in green for some reason not red or black as you would image. It was like rays of light were coming out of his head and they were streaming to all parts of the court room.

At trial the judge stated that my businesses were rogue from the beginning. That is a load of bollocks. However this is not really the fault of the judge it was the fault of my incredibly negligent or corrupt defence counsel.

Not only did the defence counsel not inform the judge and jury at trial that I was a bi polar sufferer that included psychosis but also that I was at high risk of suicide, had severe alcohol and drug problems and possible brain damage. I know that it seems incredible that they did not provide any of this information

Had the judge and jury known all of these facts then I may not have received a prison sentence at all but even if I did I do not believe it would have been more than serving 1 to 2 years in prison rather than the grossly unjustifiable 4 years.

Now out of the approximate 300 clients that I had in the wine businesses only 24 of them decided to come forward as witnesses at trial. Some of these actual 24 witnesses didn't actually lose any money in reality. Although some of their wines were not ultimately delivered due to the fraud against me by Alexander Dembinski where their wine was never delivered, they actually made some good money from the cases that they did have delivered to their government bonded accounts. As stated on that basis a good few of them in reality lost no money whatsoever and this was proven at trial

Indeed it is important to realise that millions of pounds of cases of fine wine investment stock was actually delivered In Bond to the clients personal account or cash was received by clients that had either sold the wine en primeur or sold back to us or another client whilst their stock was In Bond.

It was only due to the failing of delivery of wine by Alexander Dembinski that ultimately led to the downfall of the businesses.

When I was on the stand at trial I was questioned as to why I was putting money into a villa in Spain. I explained I was going to create a meeting place in the form of a boutique hotel that wealthy people around the world would come and stay and we could then discuss options of curing poverty around the world. I could see the jury laughing but I didn't understand why.

Ultimately I was sentenced on ten counts of fraud that gave me a sentence of 8 years in total. That's 4 to spend in Jail and the other 4 years out on probation.

Abubaker Patel

In 2017 a Barclays Bank manager that stole hundreds of thousands of pounds from his bank was not sentenced to anytime in prison. This sort of corporate theft would usually mean a 5 year prison sentence.

However Mr Patel was a Bi Polar sufferer. The trial judge said that Mr Patel was not to blame for his debilitating illness and on that basis spared him jail.

So do you see how the above example provides clarity that had I received a Fair Trial I may not have gone to prison. Mr Patel must have been of reasonable mind most of the time or he would not have been able to act as a Bank Manager. However I was not only Bi Polar, but was at high risk of suicide, and had severe alcohol and drug problems.

Not only this, but I have read an important document that submitted that 7 out of 10 victims of crime that have been carried out by someone with a mental disorder would not press charges on them. None of the 24 alleged victims new about my Mental Disorder! So in effect of the 24 victims that attended trial, 17 of those would not have acted as witnesses had they known of my Bi Polar Disorder amongst other things

If I wasn't defrauded by Alexander Dembinski then everything would have worked out fine

The Financial Account's for the business were a highly complex set of mathematics.

My pathetic legal team couldn't get their heads around the numbers.

I tried to explain to them but they couldn't understand. They instructed a highly reputable and well known forensic accountant. I went to see this accountant on a few occasions…

"Mr Constantinos" he said… "Your legal team said that you're accounts are nonsensical and don't add up"…

"Yes they do" I said… well he said I have spent a few days looking at them and I can't get my head around them'…

I spent 2 or 3 days explaining to a forensic accountant how they did work and how they made sense. He finally started to understand what he was looking at. He told me he had never seen a set of accounts organised is such a complex or unusual way…. his end analysis which took some weeks to unveil discovered that although my accounting methods were unusual and possibly not in a legal or were correct in the way that I should have run the accounting of the business, that had I not been defrauded by Alexander then everything would have worked out fine.

I recall him joking to me that if I ever needed a job in the future that he would have one for me…. I know he was joking but in effect I also knew he was quite wowed that an average bloke could have worked out my accounts not only in such a way but in that they actually worked.

However the judge said that I was too smart to have been defrauded by Alexander Dembinski. **BUT HE DIDN'T KNOW I SUFFERED WITH BI POLAR!!**

Ultimately I was found guilty on all accounts by the Jury. I was taken down to the dungeon cells of the old bailey – not even

5ft wide. I waited for my defence counsel to come and see. They came and started their bullshit excuses. I said to them 'you have completely fucked up my whole case' my defence was my Bi Polar Disorder.

The QC said "You do not suffer with Bi Polar Disorder Mr Constantinos and we could find no evidence of this" they said.

What the fuck were they talking about? This was a disaster of mega proportions.

Financial Risks

The financial risks I took where normal to me. You will have noted earlier within the book that I wrote down many of the unfortunate traits and characteristics of being a bi polar sufferer. One of these traits was 'taking financial risks'. It may appear to you when reading through what happened with the business that I took financial risks. However to have taken financial risks I would have to have known that in effect that Is what i was doing.

However I was not aware that I was taking financial risks. For me and the decisions that I made were absolutely normal and correct in my mind.

Old Bailey Summary

I absolutely did not have a Fair Trial and on that basis my conviction should be quashed. I have fully studied the law on this and there is no doubt about it. I served 4 years in Prison for a crime that I didn't even really know I was committing. If it hadn't been for the actions of Alexander Dembinski then everything would have been fine. It is true that I must have made poor decisions, took financial risks, was gullible, was led down the garden path, I was delusional and grandiose in my thinking. However at all times I believed I was doing the right thing.

Belmarsh Prison June 2015 until September 2015

A few hours later I was carted off in a prison sweatbox (van) to Belmarsh Prison. This is situated in South East London and where all convicts initially go to once sentenced by the court at the Old Bailey. Although I was found guilty on all accounts and remanded my actual sentencing wouldn't take place for another month. Your feet are chained together when you are in a sweatbox. You are put in a cubicle that is about 3ft square. The windows are blackened so you can see out but no one can see in. If you need a shit or a piss you are fucked. I was in the van with a few others. It seemed like a couple of the other lads had been to prison before so knew what to expect. They were laughing and joking. I think that they only had to do 3 or 6 months inside. Light work! I was facing 4 years behind the door.

Belmarsh is probably regarded not only as the hardest prison in the UK but also houses some of the worst criminals.

We had arrived at Belmarsh. So after being in the prisoner reception area for about 2 hours, 2 other guys and I were led to the overnight centre. These 2 guys were serving 6 months for beating someone up. We completed the necessary paperwork. Then they conducted their strip searches. One of the things they did is make you squat butt naked on top of some kind of machine that detected if there was anything hidden up your arse like drugs etc. In the months leading to this time I never really actually considered what prison would be like as I didn't believe I was going to go there. In my mind I had done nothing wrong and the court would see this. How fucking wrong I was.

3 Man Bang Up

For some reason I presumed that I would be put into a one man cell – fuck knows why. In Belmarsh you have one man bang up or 3 man bang up. The 3 man cells weren't much bigger than the one man cells. We arrived at the cell door. The guard opens the door. Fuck!...It is a 3 man bang up cell. The 3 of us were locked in the cell. There is a bunk bed on one side and a single bed on the other side. I took the lower side of one of the bunks. Luckily the 2 guys were not much younger than me and both Essex Boys also so no problems there.

I was fucking knackered by this stage. They say that you will cry in your first night in prison when you hear that door close. Did I fuck – I had no interest in crying I just wanted to go to sleep.

I was nodding off when I remembered for some reason that I should inform the 2 boys that due to my sleep apnoea I snore really badly. "Ok" they said but we will let you know. I must have fallen asleep but soon after I was woken up by the lads. "Sorry Mate", 'your snoring is Fucking ridiculous' they said. 'You sound like a fucking aeroplane' they said.

I apologised and went back to sleep. Sooner or later I could hear them banging on the cell door. 'Officer, officer' they were shouting. An officer came to the cell door. They informed him that they could not get to sleep with my super loud snoring. Luckily for them and me I was moved to another cell on the induction wing. It was a single cell. Thank fuck for that I thought!

The next morning we were taken to the proper prisoner wings. I had my 2 plastic bags of stuff and was hoping that they would put me in a single cell. Some people don't mind being in a cell with someone else. For me that would have been my worst nightmare. It's mostly the young ones that don't mind sharing but the older you get the more difficult it gets.

You need your own space, don't want to watch other men on the toilet, or smell them if they stink, or listen to them when you are tired or battle over whether you are going to watch Eastenders or fucking Coronation Street on the TV that evening.

So I got to the wing. It was association time. All of the inmates would be out of their cells. They were either playing pool, on the phone or hustling etc. The officer took me to my cell. 'There you go' he said and walked away. I walked in to the cell. 2 black guys were staring at me. 'Hey' they said in a straight face and low key voice. 'That's your bed' one of them said. He pointed to the lower bunk. Thank fuck for that. I weighed 21 stone at the time and really didn't want to be put on the top bunk. I'm pretty sure that the guy didn't want to take the chance of me being on the top bunk either lol!

I lied on my bed and for those next 5 or 10 minutes ended up being one of the worst of my time in prison. Well for psychological reasons anyway. I just presumed I would be in that cell for 4 years with these 2 other guys. There is no way I could do that without it kicking off at some time. This was when it had really sunk in where I was and how long I was going to be there for.

I day dreamed ahead to my release in 4 years' time. Then I suddenly remembered, I should warn the other guys about my sleep apnoea and snoring. So I did. I told them, they looked at me and said that I was not staying there. One of them started to shuffle my bags with his foot out of the door. He repeated 'you are not staying in here' by now my bags were out the door.

"What do I do" I said –

"Just go and tell the officer" he said – 'tell them what' I said – 'just make something up' they said.

Fuck, "what should I do now" I thought. I picked up my bags and went to the front desk. I told the officer about my snoring and sleep apnoea. "I don't give a shit" he said – 'go back to your cell'

I went back to the cell and the 2 guys are looking at me with eyes like saying "what the fuck are you doing back here".

I explained to them what had happened but they weren't having it. They started to push my bags back out of the cell again. This was now getting quite stressful. The Yard man (Jamaican) said there would be trouble if I stayed in the cell. I was stressed and annoyed.

What could I say to the officer to get me out of that cell. I walked back to the officer's desk and told him I feared for my safety if I was left in that cell. As soon as I said that he told me to grab my bags and follow him. We went up a level to the 2s (1st Floor) and he took me to a single cell.

What a fucking result I thought. It's like all of my Christmases had come at once. For that next hour I was buzzing.

I sorted my stuff out and then went to phone Ann and the kids. I told the girls that everything would be ok and that they will come and visit me soon. They were calm and fine which was the most important thing for me.

I was so fucking relieved. Anyway I had a stroll around the wing. I nodded my head a couple of times to those people that acknowledged me. I made a couple of small chit chats. I would say the wing was split as follows. 50% of inmates were black. 25% were White and the remaining mostly Pakistani or Bangladeshi. Not that it was important. I'm a bit of a 'stats' guy, I suppose it's my nature to calculate things. I got a couple of dodgy looks but nothing too serious. For that first hour I kept myself to myself and just studied my new environment.

Very soon after arriving at Belmarsh I started hearing the late night prayers by a Muslim guy who would pray to 'Allah' and call or sing out his name. He would stand by his cell window and start the prayer. Everyone on our wing at least would have been able to hear him. It was the first time I heard Muslim chanting or praying this close. I must say it was/is one of the most calming and beautiful sounds that I have ever heard.

Weight Loss

After being inside for 3 days I realised this was a good opportunity for me to lose weight. I entered prison at a weight of 20 stone 11lbs. I was a proper fat boy lol!! Some 15 months later I had lost 6 stone 9lbs taking my weight down to 14 stone 2lbs. I did it by simply eating around 300 or 400 calories less per day over this long period. I still ate most things it was just a long term calorie controlled diet. I will detail more about my weight loss later in the book.

Shower Time?

So I had now been at Belmarsh for a couple of weeks. I went downstairs to make a phone call.

I then walked back to my cell and bam!! "Where's my fucking TV gone"? Now when you misbehave in prison the officers as a form of punishment may take your TV away for a week or two and put you on something called 'Basic'…. But I hadn't done anything wrong! I knew then that someone who was already on basic and had no TV must have stolen mine!

This happens all the time but is pointless as the culprit is always found out. I stormed out of my cell and vociferously put the word out to find out who had nicked it!! I started looking in peoples cells which pissed some people off and got close to a fight on a couple of occasions within a few minutes. Sooner or later I found out who had taken it. I got it back and thought that was that.

A little while later I got a message that the guy who had stolen it wanted a meet up in the shower. Now I had only been in prison for a few weeks so didn't really know what 'meeting in the shower room' actually meant in prison terms.

It meant that you are going to have a straightener… a fight!

The guy was pissed off because he thought I made a big deal out of the situation. I started walking to the shower. He was 10 yards in front of me with his mate. I just thought we were going to have a civil chat about the situation. However the other 2 guys were going there for other reasons!! So we arrived at the shower and I confidently confronted them…

"Hello boys"… 'what's up' I said.

The guys looked a little setback and confused. We discussed the situation then I left… simple no problems. 10 minutes later one of the 'top boys' on the wing came to my cell … we called him 'Fifty' as he looked like film and music star 50 cents.

"Looks like you handled that well" he said to me.

"What do you mean" I said…he told me the 2 guys wanted to meet me in the shower room for a fight…apparently one of them had a shank on them. Really … fuck…well it turned out that because I entered the shower room oozing with confidence it scared the guys off. They presumed that I would have known the meet up was for a straightener… but luckily because I didn't, I had no stress about the situation which scared them off… Fucking hell I got away with that one!

Corruption in the UK Justice System

So a few weeks into my time at Belmarsh I was mulling over my unfair trial and the blatant negligence or worse that had been placed on me by my trial defence counsel. I knew that there was an appeal process. I informed the Solicitors that we should appeal as they fucked my whole defence up. They said they would look into it. On the last day of a possible appeal the wanker solicitor sent me a letter that I had no grounds for appeal as there could find no evidence of Bi Polar Disorder.

Now they were just taking the Piss!

They had pages upon pages of confirmations. They were just mugging me off. It was quite incredible. How could they actually think that they could get away with this deceit? It was so scandalous they must have been stupid to think that they could get away with it. Well they almost did but it would take a very long time before they would be held accountable for their actions. As previously mentioned, my next book which will hopefully be released in January 2024 will cover this topic in detail. I believe at this stage and time of writing the book will be called **'Corruption within the UK Justice System'**.

My appeal time was over and I had no solicitor. I had no idea what to do next.

Dave and the Archbold

However after a few weeks of being in Belmarsh prison a guy called Dave moved into the cell next to me. A mixed race guy in his late 50s I suppose. We started chatting and before you know it the question comes out that all inmates ask each other…'what are you in for'.

He was in for some kind of credit card fraud. We got chatting and he told me that he was going to appeal his sentence which was for 6.5 years. He had already started writing out his appeal.

He was using lots of legal jargon and references of laws that were in the British book of law.

This book is called 'The Archbold'

"How the Fuck do you know all this stuff" I said to him?

He said "Read the Archbold". At that time I had no idea what the Archbold was.

I asked Dave to help me write an appeal even though I was out of time but there was only so much he could do to help me.

He said that I was allowed 1 session a week in the library to use the Archbold to help me with any case for appeal etc. It was a chance to study the law surrounding my case.

So I booked the earliest opportunity to go to the library.

"Can I have a copy of the Archbold" I said to the librarian… she handed me the book. Fuck me… this was one of the biggest books I had ever seen. It must have had close to 1000 words per page and over 2000 pages…. That's 2 million words inside it!!

I knew very little at this time about law. Imagine seeing a book with 2 million words in it and knowing that only small parts of it were relevant to you and that those small parts were scattered throughout the book.

Now to make it even more difficult I didn't even know what it was exactly that I was looking for.

I began studying the Archbold. I would take copies of certain pages. I would learn what I could in the Library with the time that was allotted to me. A month had passed and things started to make sense to me.

It was becoming clear that my trial was a complete fuck up and that my sentence at least should be quashed and maybe even my conviction. There was an Abuse of process and the trial defence counsel omitted key information plus much more. I started to clearly see that I had a solid case for appeal. **My pathway to obtain justice had begun**.

I had only spent in total around 2.5 month at Belmarsh prison, but it was quite amazing what each new day would bring. There was always something to gossip about.

For example, you would see someone on the front page of the paper one day and the next day he would be at Belmarsh. A particular guy I remember was on the front page for beating his wife to death. The next day he was in the cell opposite me. I was already starting to get a bit of a name after a couple of months at Belmarsh of being the Jailhouse legal advisor.

This guy who killed his wife came to me after a couple of days and wanted some help on understanding on what grounds he could appeal. I really didn't feel comfortable in helping a guy that had just murdered his wife so I swerved the situation.

First Visit

It had been 3 weeks since I had seen my kids. I was sitting in the visiting hall with great excitement and anticipation. I could see nervousness in some of the other inmates waiting for their families. Then there they were. My Sister, Ann, Sophia and Elena were walking through the entrance. Elena who was only 10 years old at the time spotted me straight away and ran towards me. She literally jumped on me. She started crying. I was holding back the tears. I hugged all 4 of them. I spent most of the visit reassuring my daughters that daddy would be out soon and they had nothing to worry about. Etc etc.

Luckily for me throughout my whole time inside Ann would bring the girls to see me once a month. I am so thankful to her for this. Some inmates don't get to see their children at all. That would have been devastating for me. I needed to see them and they needed to see me.

I especially enjoyed the special family visits that I would be allowed at Wayland Prison from time to time. These visits were for just maybe 7 inmates at a time and where the whole visiting hall would be made available for just us 7 and our families. The hall would have loads of games, toys and activities to keep the children occupied with. These visits would last for 4 hours. It was a very precious time. I needed to see my daughters. I needed to show them that everything was ok. They needed to see their dad. Psychologically it was a massive thing for me. Without these kinds of visits I am sure that my mental health would have deteriorated even more rapidly.

Chris

My first proper mate at Belmarsh prison was a black guy in his early 20s called Chris from one of the hoods in South London. We got on well, both loved football… he was a Manchester United fan. We both worked in this shitty factory job for a while sorting out CDs… fucking boring. He was only in for a short time and literally only had a couple of months left… lucky bastard. Back then before they put phones in individual cells there would be 6 phones in the social area of the wing to cover 60 to 80 inmates. You would have to queue up to use the phone. This was often a point for argument. Some guys would try and push in and if you were on the phone too long you would hear the guys in the queue moaning and groaning to hurry you up.

One time this guy was taking too long. A big guy from the queue came up to the front took the phone off the guy who was on a call … smacked him over the head with it and made his call. There was blood spurting out this poor guy's nose and he was sent to the medical unit…what a fucking liberty. Shocking to see and angered me but there was fuck all I could do about it.

One time Chris was in the queue for the phone. One of the lifers turned up and stated that he was in front of Chris. They had a disagreement and Chris held his own. Now Chris literally only had a few days left if his sentence. Getting into a fight with a lifer at this stage of his sentence would be beyond stupid… Can you imagine all of the possible consequences! In a fight! I went up to Chris and in front of them I purposely sided with the other guy

"Hey guys come on"… 'Chris your' going home in a few days just let the guy make his call'

I was looking at Chris with screwed eyes trying to send a message to trust me on this one. Chris backed off … I explained to him why I done what I did and he understood.

Chris shared a cell with 2 guys. One of the guys was in for raping his niece… Chris was sick to the stomach and fuming. We all hate fucking woman beaters and nonce's (bacons, paedophiles). Once Chris found out he started losing the plot. He said he was going to do him over…imagine sharing a cell with a fucking nonce.

The problem with A/B category prisons… even if you are a C or D category prisoner when you get sentenced and first go to prison you have to go to a B category prison. So even if your crime is white colour like minor theft etc you might have to share a cell with a murderer or a rapist or a nonce.

That can't be right! …. Anyway Chris and one or two others were getting ready to give the nonce a beating. Somehow word got through to the screws that then immediately moved the guy out of the cell to a separate wing opposite us.

That backfired on him and the screws though as literally as soon as he moved into his new cell he was lynched by about 10 other inmates that gave him a good beating.

Category A – Neighbours of Evil

Sometimes, when we were on the square concrete yard at Belmarsh for exercise, you could look across to the category 'A' block. This is where some of the worst criminals in the UK are held. It looks a bit like an aeroplane hangar, but totally made of concrete. There are no windows.

Sometimes the scum that were held there would be allowed out for exercise. They would be taken to a secluded area. However they would have to pass our yard. They weren't close … at least a 100ft away…then abuse would start… many inmates would shout out 'die you fucking bacons' etc… the word 'bacons' comes from bacon bonce which rhymes with nonce which is a slang term for a paedophile. Watching those guys chained up knowing that they would never leave prison was quite surreal. You would just stare at them and wonder what atrocities that they had got up to. Their feet would initially have been chained together. I think I would rather be dead than be in some of their shoes.

You know I spent 2.5 months in Belmarsh Prison. Was it as bad as I thought? Pretty much but I wasn't subjected to any bullying there. I was losing weight rapidly. I found an angle to appeal my case and I got so see my kids on 2 occasions.

Wayland Prison September 2015 until June 2019

So it was time to go to Wayland prison… me and one other guy. We got in the sweat box van … get shackled and locked up into a little cubicle. So a tedious 2.5 hour drive to Wayland in what was itself a very small prison cell… hey at least we could look at the window.

So we got to Wayland Prison ….they checked us in and a little while later they took us to the landing on A wing where new arrivals go. We start walking up a staircase on the wing and either side is lined with resident inmates.

They are staring at us and the odd guy shouts something out… they are trying to intimidate us… but up the stairs we go saying nothing… then one guy shouts out

"Which prison have you come from" 'Norwich' he said… I looked at him

"No" I said … 'Belmarsh'… As soon as I said that there was like a parting of the waves. They all stepped back let us through and they didn't say another word..

This put the resident inmates on the back foot as they did not know what to expect from us that is, coming from the Notorious Belmarsh Prison.…

So a couple of days after arriving at Wayland… I was moved to another part of 'A' wing and the Scottish guy who travelled up with me from Belmarsh was moved to 'C' wing.

This other part of 'A' wing is where I would be settling for the foreseeable future. There was for the most part a good set of lads there which made my time easier.

So as usual the other guys would ask you what you were in for… ok so "fraud" ……'Investment fraud' i said.

"How much did you make" they said…

"Oh not that much" … 'just maybe a few hundred grand' I said. It was actually £10M!!

You will have learned in this book it was actually a lot more than that.… I didn't want to state the correct amount as that could draw unwanted attention… I had heard stories whilst in Belmarsh of people that had made a lot of money through their alleged crimes could be victims of gangs who would threaten you and try and get you to make arrangements with someone on the outside to transfer these gangs money.

£100,000 **or** £10 Million

Anyway a couple of months had passed and I had a good few mates on the wing now. One of them was Russell, a mixed race guy from Islington. Big Arsenal fan as you would expect coming from Islington… sorry whilst we are on the subject of Islington… I found it quite extraordinary how many prisoners at Wayland came from that area…loads of them….. any way… Russell and I would joke about our alleged crimes….Although he was sentenced for suspicion of conspiracy to armed robbery… I used to wind him saying he was a 2 bob street corner drug dealer… so I nicknamed him 2 bob… now this guy was a weightlifter and as fit as fuck so luckily for me he could take the banter otherwise he could have battered me lol…

He took it all in good humour…anyway one day we were having a bit of banter again… usually Tottenham v Arsenal banter… but this particular day Russell said to me "So remind me again how much money you done in your investment business"

I said "around £300,000"….

He said "I bet you didn't and laughed" …

I said "what" …

He said "I bet you it was more like £100,000" … tops!

I laughed back… "What makes you think that" I said…

He said "I just have a feeling you are bullshitting the amount".

So there were a few other lads standing about and the banter went on for a while…then I said "Hold on guys"… 'I've not been telling you the truth'… so they were waiting for the news that actually it was a much lower amount than the £300,000 that I initially said… instead I told them the truth…."I done £10M" I said… they burst out laughing.

They were thinking, who is this deluded guy. However as they seemed so shocked when I said £10m and none of them believed me at the time… I played along with it

I gave the impression that I might be lying but also did it in such a way that some started thinking "I don't know you know"… 'this guy might be a bit smarter than we give him credit for'.

Anyway the banter carried on for a couple of days with more people starting to believe in the £10M figure… I was toiling with Russell and he changed his mind and raised the amount to now believing I had done £1M but 'There is no way you have hustled £10M'….

So by now the whole of our landing was involved in the banter… at first I refused to show any of my legal paperwork confirming what the real amount was… but it was getting to crunch time…."I bet you £50 on the canteen that it is no more than £1M" Russell said…

"£100 on the canteen that it's £10M" I said.

The whole landing erupted with noise and gestures as to who was right…. Was I telling the truth?

So the bet was £100… that's a small fortune in prison… you could live like a king for at least a month…everyone gathered round, I went to my cell to get the legal paperwork that would prove it one way or the other…. I handed the paperwork to 2 of the lads… I looked at Russell with a smile on my face … he looked at me with a smile on his but he was a bit nervy… the guys looked at the paperwork….

A few seconds passed then there were shouts…. "Raaaaaa… .'wow'….Jesus"….

"The fucker done £10M man"...I was applauded like a hero... Russell couldn't believe it....

"You dodgy bastard" he said and laughed... I think it was nice to see that even the big man on the wing could sometimes lose... Russell took it well and paid most of the canteen money that I won, over the next few weeks... I stopped taking the money I reckon when I had received about £70... that was enough for me

"What you in for mate"

As previously mentioned... when you arrive at prison you are always asked what you are in for by the other inmates? So you tell them.... Unless you are a rapist or woman beater or nonce... which if you are, you are informed by officers that you should make another story up. This is common sense anyway, unless you like the idea of getting beaten the fuck out of!

Usually though sooner or later you would get found out. Towards the end of my sentence some guy in my wing gave out the names of almost all the inmates on our wing to a friend on the out to investigate who had really done what. Most of it was as thought and as explained by the individual inmate. However there were one or two shockers.

We discovered that one guy who claimed he got in a fight in Spain, hit another guy who fell and banged his head and was killed...... Actually what had happened was that he was on holiday in Spain with his girlfriend... got jealous as he thought she was flirting with another guy....then beat her to death....He put her in a black plastic bag of some sort and dumped her in the sea!!!... Scum bag.

Legal work continued

Wayland had a good library and it was probably the most pleasant place in the whole prison. The mind set of prisoners was different in there. It was like a calming place and the closest place to normality that the prison could offer you. You could have been in any library anywhere.

I used to frequent the library at least once a week at Wayland prison. The Library was managed by a lovely lady called Sarah. She was a massive Robbie Williams fan… somewhat obsessed by him lol!! Many of her conversations would somehow include the name Robbie Williams wherever possible. The library was my engine room of hope that someday I could get justice. I wrote letters upon letters to the Court of Appeal and the CCRC but they were ignored or their responses were clearly evasive and in effect their only interest was their bias so as to protect my criminal legal team. The corruption was so scandalous you will be astonished when you read their responses which will be published in my next book.

Sexy Beast

Once we got half way through 2016 I went to the gym quite regularly. I was started to look really good, fit and athletic, 6ft tall and tanned….it's true that the female officers voted me as one if the top 5 sexiest blokes in the prison. I went from fat bastard to sexy in 15 months…. Anyway that didn't last too long, the weight started creeping up slowly again. However for the period of time it felt good. I lost just short of 100 lbs in weight. However, then I put a load back on but now I have lost a fair amount again. I am sure lots of you out there have been in similar situations. However, my problem at the moment is not eating excess food but is the alcohol that consume

New Fine Wine Investment Business!

So people knew I was in for fraud… and soon realised it was for quite a lot of money. As you now know it was in the millions. People wanted to know exactly what I done and how I supposedly done it. People wanted me to teach them so that upon their release they could go out and do it themselves…fucking hell… firstly I wasn't going to do that and secondly in my mind I hadn't actually defrauded anyone.

However, there was no point telling them that as they wouldn't have believed me. A few of them wanted me to run a daily fucking course in our break time teaching them the ins and outs of everything on how to set up and run a wine investment business… they would pay me with goods from the canteen… I laughed… "boys, I ain't doing it" …. They were so eager to find out how to make real fucking money, they couldn't control themselves…

Most people in a Category C prison are in for minor drug dealing offences or some kind of theft. For a lot of these guys it was there 5th plus time in prison. I found this incredible. I don't know how they could keep coming back to jail. Surely once was enough. Many of these are career criminals. As far as they are concerned, why would they get a shit paid normal job if they can hit a jewellery shop a couple of times a year and make up to £100,000 each.

Or make potentially similar money by selling weed or cocaine. They always thought that they wouldn't get caught again but eventually they usually would. I would rather remain on government benefits for the rest of my life rather than risking going back into a prison. What a fucking waste of life.

2 Hours until Fight Time

When I first moved to Wayland prison I was on 'A' wing. There were some good guys on that wing and we had some laughs. Especially, Tottenham v Arsenal banter. However there was this one guy that was in the cell next to me, he had emotional problems due to losing his mum whilst he was inside.

He was always triggering an argument with someone. He liked to play fight… the guy was in his early 40s… generally it was the lads in their early 20s that had play fights so it was a bit weird. One day we had a proper argument and it was very close to kicking off but the cell doors were about to be slammed closed for 2 hour lock up at lunch. We went into our cells. A guy looked through the flap on my cell door and gave me the message that my neighbour was coming for me as soon as the cell doors open at 2 after lunch…. ok!…. It looks like I was going to have my first fight in prison. I felt quite nervy as you do not know what to expect.

It was 2 o'clock and the cell doors opened. I was bouncing on my feet waiting for the guy to charge into my cell. He never turned up. I walked out onto the landing and he was nowhere to be seen. I had just spent 2 hours in my cell psyching myself up for nothing. Well that's good. It's always better to avoid a fight if you can. Especially in prison as it is too risky.

Constantinou Brothers

After being at Wayland prison for a few weeks a guy came up to me from my wing…

"I see your surname is Constantinos" he said looking at me straight in the face.

"Yes" I said….

"Do you know the Constantinou brothers from Camden/Archway" he replied

My first thoughts were why is he asking me that… could be dodgy… maybe he had a beef with them! If he thought I was related to then in some way it could be trouble for me!

I said to him "I'm not sure"… turns out that he was good mates with them. Apparently the brothers were quite notorious in the London Underworld.

I just played along with it and said it was possible but not sure. Turns out that over the years in prison several guys from the Islington and Camden areas all asked me the same question… clearly these guys were well known. I don't know… maybe if they read this book or anyone knows them… they can get in contact with me… would be good to meet relatives that I hadn't ever seen or at least not see since I was a kid.

Oh ok…. Well my granddad had about 10 brothers and sisters that many of whom moved to the UK from Cyprus in the 1950s. They all settled in the Archway area of North London. The brothers as I said were from that area. On the basis it is quite conceivable that they were related to me. I hadn't seen any of those relatives from Archway since I was a kid so I didn't really remember for sure if I had met or was related to the 2 brothers.

Anyway having them as a 'possible' relative whilst I was in prison gave me some kind of respect and on some occasions possibly held me in good stead as a prisoner

Shank

In prison you hear the words "I'm going Shank man up" almost every day. A shank for those of you that don't know is a prison made weapon that is made with a sharp end that enables an inmate to cut or stab another person. You will be shocked at the sort of shanks that can be created. At times when seeing some of the weapons that had been made, i was surprised as to where they found the materials from to make the shank. There are so many in prison it is a miracle that there are not more injuries or death. Many prisoners make one in the form of protection rather than attack purposes.

Often when a fight breaks out the 2 inmates for example will lock themselves' in a cell. You will invite the guy you have 'beef' with into your cell and the door will be slammed shut. It can be worrying though to go into someone else's cell as they may have a shank in there…. It's crazy shit… when they are used, most of the time they are used to cut a person's face up rather than stab them.

Real Insanity – Mad Man

There was one guy on my wing that was totally insane… I mean totally, not bouts of insanity like bi polar but 100 per cent mentally not there. He never came out of his cell and we were not sure if he was allowed out of his cell.

He never spoke and just mumbled. Every now and again an inmate would look into the guy's cell. He would always be naked and excrement thrown all over his cell.

We use to question the screws why he was in a normal prison …. He should be in a mental institution… they agreed but it was some weeks before he was shipped out.

In the meantime he used to fill a bucket up with his urine and pour it through the small gap at the bottom of his cell door flooding the landing. We had to put up with it and clear it up ourselves.

The guy would say very little other than "you fucking niggas" a few times a day which at first the black guys on the wing thought was funny but after a while it really started to piss them off.

They would go to the mad man's cell and threaten him and one occasion enticed the guy to bang his head against the wall. When the guy actually started doing just that they stopped as they realised he was truly insane.

Real Insanity – The IPP Sentence

Another extremely concerning thing that I found in prison was people that were prisoners under the IPP law. This hugely fucked up law was in effect a mental torture weapon… that's how it panned out anyway.

So what this sentence meant is that for example you were sentenced for the offence of burglary… ok… usually in the past you would just get a straight forward sentence for example 6 years… serve 3 years inside and then 3 years' probation on the outside.

Some completely out of the real world politician changed the ruling of the sentence to as follows. Serve 3 years in prison and then if the parole team and any psychiatrists and prison workers all agreed that the prisoner was now 'cured' of their crime committing they would then give the go ahead for release.

The problem was that none of these parties would want to instigate a sign off for release as they feared if the convict committed another crime the blame could fall back on them. So no one would sign the paperwork off blaming this and that bullshit reason… 'Oh he has mental issues'…. Or 'he has not done enough courses'… just utter none sense. The prisoner and his family would be left mentally tortured… where they thought he would be incarcerated for 3 years a prisoner could often as I witnessed spend 10 years plus in prison. What a bloody disgrace! Imagine being that dad and his kids who want to be together but waiting year after year for release never knowing when it's going to happen. This is absolute mental torture and the people who put this sentence in place should be sacked and actually imprisoned for coming up with such a disgusting law.

There was a guy just a couple of cells down from me on C Wing. He was on this IPP sentence. It was a similar situation. He was due out after being inside for 3 years but had been imprisoned for 11 years!! Shocking… you could see he was being mentally tortured and that time was making him behave worse due to his frustration.

So it was like a catch 22 situation…he would smoke spice to relieve his anger and get in trouble every now and again but there were always some reasons or another they wouldn't allow him to go home. At the time I left, he had been in prison for almost 4 times longer than he should have been.

He got to a stage where to gain some attention to his plight he would cut the inside of his mouth mainly inside if his cheeks. Seriously do you know how much blood splatter this can cause? He use to fill all walls in his cell with blood that used to jet out of his mouth like hoses... incredible and scary to think what one would do in their desperation to try and make the authorities realise what they were doing to him.

Screws

Now believe it or not most prison screws are ok... you behave and you have no issues with them. However there were' a handful that could be a right bunch of dick-headed wankers! You feel that some of these nasty officers must have been bullied or something similar when they were younger.

They liked their prison officer jobs mainly as it allowed them to mistreat inmates. I believe they must feel it is like some kind of revenge that they are inflicting on others to compensate what may have happened to them in the past. The worst ones would love to give a beating to an inmate that misbehaved... they could get away with it.... We'll certainly most of the time.

I remember on one occasion that one inmate was having an argument with one of the screws. The screw contacted the main office for help... another 4 screws turned up. It seemed like the inmate was making a valid argument about something... but the screws just started intimidating him... moving forward like they were going to attack him.

The inmate panicked and just pushed out his arms to hold them back.... Just because of that the 5 screw fuckers started laying into him…dropped him to the ground… hands behind back and handcuffed him… before they lifted him to his feet a couple of them put a boot in to his ribs and his face which was totally illegal, cowardly, dangerous and totally un-fucking necessary… bunch of melts…

Now there were a lot of other prisoners that saw this happen… I swear down it was a really close situation that a riot would have broken out due to what the officers did… it was touch and go… if it had gone off there would have been serious blood-shed. What a fucking liberty!

Duncan

There was a guy in his mid to late 50s… a small chap, only about 5ft tall… long greyish beard… and long greasy ageing hair…he was a bit of a wild one but one of the funniest guys I ever met whilst being inside.

Unfortunately for him he had spent 35 years of his life behind the door. Not all in one stretch but continued minor offending kept sending back again and again etc.

He never worked, rarely left his cell and wasn't allowed a TV due to his refusal to work. He occupied himself by reading and sleeping! Now this guy was quite smart but he had a problem with alcohol on the outside that always caused problems.

In prison, he had in the past experienced several bad occasions like getting beat up in the showers due to some of his white supremacy tattoos. He would never shower as he feared that the same could happen again and instead used the wash basin in his cell. I could not get my head around as to how and why he allowed himself to be imprisoned time and time again… spending most of his life behind the door… it's just a shame what a waste of a life..

Self-Harm

One of the saddest things you will see in prison and there are many sad things are those that self-harm. This is usually done by using a razor blade to cut your arms… usually one or 2 inch cuts in length with a deep enough cut to leave a scar. There are some guys with hundreds of these cuts. Why do they do it? I'm not sure anyone knows but the theory is that they do it to somehow relieve mental pain whilst being locked up. Others are trying to send a message to the establishment that they are need of help. What a terrible thing to have to live with.

When you see the scars on some of these guys it makes you cringe. What kind of destitute place are they in their mind to do this to themselves. My daily pain on the other hand was waiting to see if my daughters were Ok…….

1500 days x 'Are my daughters OK'?

Imagine, I was behind the door for 4 years which is roughly 1500 days. I have a deep fear of loss due to losing both my parents on the car accident when I was 14 years old. So every day I would worry if my kids were ok. I had a profound fear that something would happen to them. I would call them every day but the anticipation of waiting to hear that they were ok when calling them was highly stressful. As soon as they answered I would quickly ask "are you ok" …'is your sister ok' then a huge sigh of relief. I know that they can't always have been ok but they knew about my stress and played down or avoided as best they could any issues they might have had to protect me. But once again imagine going through that every day for 1,500 days! No wonder I've got very little fucking hair!

Angels

It had been quite a few years now since I had seen the Angels. I laid there on my bed most night hoping and waiting they would come and visit me. I did now know what I was supposed to be doing yet to help the world. What could I do stuck in prison? They never visited me again whilst I was inside.

However, around the time of My Amazing Grace moment which was a year or so after my release, I did see them again as you will see later.

'Oh Lord My Troubles are Hard'

One evening … I think it was on C wing, we were all banged up for the evening. It must have been about 7pm and most of the guys would have been watching Eastenders on the TV. Now there are two corridors on each side of each wing that form like an 'L' shape. In each 'L' shape there would be about 40 prisoners. If someone shouted out to you on one side of your part of the L shape you could easily hear them on the other side.

On this particular evening I could hear one of the brothers a few doors down singing. I know something bad had happened in his family in the recent days and he just wasn't himself. He was not singing overly loud but I could hear his words which appear to come from a well know song….

"Oh Lord my troubles are hard…. Oh Lord my troubles are hard… don't you know Lord that my troubles are hard.. don't you know Lord that my troubles are hard" he had a beautifully soothing voice…

Then shortly after another inmate would join in then another and another… before you knew it, the whole of our side of C wing were singing the song altogether in perfect synchrony… it was amazing… this must have gone on for about 10 minutes… then it fell silent … not one person said another word… nothing at all, no shouting out… it just stopped and went completely silent… it was a wonderful comforting moment. The brotherhood of we caged animals just for that short moment in time felt to us like we were all as one, as brothers. We were powerful…

Highly Intelligent

So about 2 years into my sentence I started one of the courses that I needed to do as part of my time. I believe it had to do with addictions like alcohol etc. I met the teacher. She had my notes so she would have known a lot about me. During a conversation she revealed that she knew I was a bi polar sufferer and that she worked with bi polar sufferers in a previous job.

Bi polar sufferers are so intelligent' she said… "I wish I was bi polar" she said! Can you believe she did actually say that? What the fuck I thought!

There are some benefits like having a creative mind but surely she cannot have understood all the negative traits and characteristics that bi polar sufferers have to deal with. I found it very strange that she would say something like that.

Torture followed by madness then Suicide

My cell on fire… I used to think about hanging myself. It was a 'pill' suicide attempt.

In September 2017 I took an overdose of my medication. I cannot say for sure it was a suicide attempt but on the face of it, it appears so. Many of my tablets had been consumed and I did not feel well at all. For a while after that I was prevented from keeping hold of my own medication. I was kept at close watch for a couple of days. I had been in prison far too long than my Bi Polar mind could handle. I was being mentally tortured and pushed to the limit.

I somehow recall that the days leading up to that event were very depressing for me.

I believe I would often hallucinate. On one occasion I believed I was back in the car at the accident when I was 14. The car - (prison cell) was on fire and I couldn't get out… I felt I was burning… I started banging on the cell door… "Let me out I'm on fire"…

I heard 'The Rock' (my mate) in the cell next door shouting out – "what's going on", 'Spyros mate what the fuck'… it seems as soon as he said my name I snapped out of whatever hallucinogenic state that I was in. It was terrifying… an officer soon arrived.

I got to meet a couple of other Bi polar Sufferers whilst at Wayland Prison. One guy called Sol was someone I chatted to every now and again. I didn't see much of him as he was on another wing. One day I bumped into him. He had a thick mark going round his neck. He had tried to hang himself the day before.

On another occasion a young guy in the cell next to me tried to hang himself. He had kept himself locked in his cell for a couple of weeks leading up to the attempted suicide. This is because he owed people money for drugs purchased. He couldn't pay so he kept himself locked up in his cell to save himself from a black eye or a beating.

He wanted to get moved to another prison for his own safety. Nothing was happening though… this sent him over the top. He started barricading. This is when you move all of your cell furniture to the entrance of the cell door… bed, table, cupboard etc. You then position it in a way so that the officers cannot enter the cell as the furniture is backed up against the other wall so there is a jam. The only way to get in is to unhinge the door and take it off… the screws were alerted and initially tried to talk him out of it.

The inmate shouts out "if you don't get me out of the prison I'm going to string up" (hang himself)… the officers were making no progress so they called the specialist team that deals with such events and who are able to take off the cell door.

So this is happening right next to me so I could hear everything that is going on. The specialist team arrive. As soon as they started the process of taking off the cell door I could hear a rush of panic in their voices… the guy had attached his rolled up bed sheet to the metal frame of the light support on the ceiling….I started banging on the wall… "Hey son what you doing"… 'stop being stupid and just open the fucking door'.

I heard panic in the voices of the screws …. I believed from what they were saying that he had tied the noose around his neck and then jumped off his bed… he was hanging…the screws were shouting … I'm waiting …'get that fucking door open' I shouted… sooner or later they did…we never saw or heard from the guy again… we don't know I if he died or was saved…or moved to another prison… we were never told.

Parole

From my experience Parole is often a load of bollocks. Let's say that you get a 15 year sentence before Parole is allowed. The view is that if you behave for those 15 years you will be allowed out after 15 years …. Right? …. Wrong!… if you think that's how it works then let me tell you - the way it works is often predetermined with regards to your release- if you get 15 years for example…..

Parole officers are already making their mind up to let you out after 18 or 20 years. So you fight to be the best you can every day for 15 years only to hear some bollocks reason that you can't be released yet because you are not a 'cured' man as such. Imagine being that guy that does everything right and you count down year by year only to be in effect punched in the face at your parole hearing… how do you think that would make you feel?… after waiting all of those years… you have to wait more years… you don't know when or if you are ever getting out. I'm not sure about the concept of parole. Maybe it would be better that you get a straight sentence… let's say 10 years or 20 years and that's what you serve unless your behaviour during that time is really bad… small tranches of months let's say could be added on for anything bad that you do whilst inside.

I'm telling you that those people that are on a sentence with Parole are mentally tortured and when they are refused their parole often for no good reason it can send them over the top.

I knew 2 people who died literally when their parole was refused. I think one was suicide but the other died let's say of natural causes.

Due to the stress of the situation his body gave up on him.

Punish criminals…. Yes OK… but they don't have to live like animals… God does not want this of his children.

Overcrowding

It humours but also saddens me the misrepresentation you may often read about in the press with regards to over-crowding in UK prisons.

Now the prison population in the UK at last count was about 85,000 people but with only a total capacity of 86,000.

You will read UK crime is out of control, our prisons are bursting…. Bla bla bla

So now let me tell you why the prisons are literally full to the limits…. Because that's how the government wants it to be!

Imagine for example there were only 50,000 prisoners…. The work load for lawyers, solicitors, barrister, parole officers, prisons officers etc would be a lot less. Less legal persons would be needed as there would be less work to do. Those in charge of the UK legal system want the prisons to be full so that all of their affiliates within the brotherhood of the UK Justice system are fed with work so that they can make more money.

This is probably why the IPP sentence was created in order to keep prisoners behind the door for longer.

Imagine if prisons worked and everyone after completing a sentence became rehabilitated and there were no more crimes and therefore no more prisoners, what would, judges, lawyers, solicitors, barristers etc, etc do? It is in the interest of the UK Justice system to keep people coming to prison

Do you see what I mean?

Black Eye Friday

Welcome to Black eye Friday! Every Friday in prison was a day when some inmates lose their dignity and receive in effect self-inflicted injury due to their desire to have access to and smoke 'spice'. Spice is a drug.

So generally there are 2 ways of paying for your Spice. Firstly someone you know on the outside transfer's money to the bank account of the dealer inside. The dealer checks with a friend on the out to see the money has come in. The dealer then gives the inmate the spice… simple!!

The other way is to buy the dealer whatever items he wants from the canteen sheet. The canteen sheet is a list of a few hundred grocery products or so that you can purchase on a weekly basis.

You can use either the money that you have earned that week at work in the prison… maybe about £20 and also up to £25 per week from money you received from friends or family.

So theoretically if you received both amounts, you could easily be getting up to £50 per week which you can spend on the canteen. Now that may not sound a lot but I can assure you that £50 a week to spend in prison is fucking loads… you would be living like a king! Lol.

So if you were buying let's say £20 of spice from the dealer, the dealer would ask you to buy certain products from your canteen sheet to the value of £20… simple…. but not always.

Some buyers would fake their canteen sheet to the dealer for it to appear that they are ordering the goods that they require for that £20 spice hit.

So Friday would come - this was canteen stock delivery day -

the dealer has eagerly got his eye on his customers. They know full well that some of the buyers may not be able to deliver on the deal.

The bullshit excuses come out....that isn't going to help you... It's Black Eye Friday time!

Smack... a full blown punch straight in the face over your eye...by Friday evening there would always be at least 2 or 3 lads with proper shiners walking around each wing. Seriously some of the black eyes received were so bad you thought that they could lose their eyesight.

Fucking sickening... but what made it even worse is that for example some guy's black eye had barely fully recovered but the stupid fucker would do it again... smash another black eye... do these guys want to lose their fucking eyesight over a bit of zombie weed?

Some guys who couldn't pay their debt would lock themselves behind the door for day's even weeks on end, never coming out to save themselves from a beating or black eye Friday.

They would move to another wing where you would think it would be safer for them.... Not at all... everyone knows everyone practically and a dealer would always have mates on all wings who would do the black eye job for them....for a price of course!

Spice Boys

It's bad enough being in prison let alone being on Spice as well as for so many reasons!

Spice oh dear.... Where do I start! So about 10 years ago I believe a new drug started arriving in the UK prisons. This drug is the mother of all fucked up drugs. Initially people would bring it in by 'banking' it. This means putting in it in some kind of container and sticking it up your arse. New prisoners would bring it in that way. Another way was for it to be handed over to you is on a visit by a relative or a friend.

Obviously this is done extremely discreetly. Women would store it in their woman bits down below. They would wear short skirts and no nickers so that they could pull the container out.... This would happen all the time .... Sometimes people would be caught but sometimes they wouldn't!

Spice which is also referred to in prison as 'Rice' or 'Mamba' looks a bit like weed and similar in colour.

But it's effect on you is totally different. For most it is a paralysing zombie kind of effect. I never smoked it but i was surrounded by it all the time as a large portion of inmates would smoke it.

Basically it appears that the drug paralysis you into some kind of weird statue form. Arms could be out like a zombie... legs slightly crouched...you can't speak... froth at the mouth.

Seriously, when there was a lot of it about people were knocking on deaths door with the amount that they were taking. On occasions you would walk onto your wing and it would be like a scene from a horror movie... zombies staggering around everywhere... people making funny noises... guys standing around naked not knowing what the fuck they were doing... ambulances arriving... 'Man down' people would shout...heart attacks would happen...like a scene from hell.... But then it got worse.

Some clever fuckers formulated a new kind of spice...it was a clear spice paste as such where you could dip sheets of paper into it. This chemical could be something like Alloy cleaner.

They would let the paper dry and somehow you could not trace that it had now in fact turned to spice paper sheets, unless you had the nose of a dog!

So now spice was flying into prison by Royal Mail… people would send letters to the prisoners from the outside… these letters would be covered with the 'Spice' alloy liquid.

If you received a good delivery of 4 or 5 sheets of paper (in the form of a letter) you could easily make a couple of bags (£2000).

The paper would be cut up into ID card sizes… and the cost for that would be £50. Just having a smoke from a tenth of an ID sized piece of paper would get people smashed.

The paper spice was getting out of control people were going over all the time. Seriously when a film is made on this book you will see the scene of what it was like on occasions.

The prison was in a state of crisis…they started getting their sniffer dogs to smell the letters/post and sooner or later the screws got a better control of it…however some still got through.

Sometimes when you see other inmates 'on it' you didn't know whether to piss yourself laughing… it really is quite funny to see someone in a Spice state… or worry that they were about to drop dead and you wasn't sure what to do… utter madness!

I've seen people eat shit in order to get a fix of spice and lick days old food splattered against the wall. I am being fucking serious.

Some brain dead fuck heads would do anything to get their fix. This is where you have to be careful. A stereotypical spice head in a UK prison is often a white person that is frail and weak. However these fuckers can be the most dangerous. If someone puts a hit out on you due to some beef they are likely to pay one of these guys with spice to do a job.

What has become of a man who smokes spice knowing that he is poisoning himself and with every drag he tempts the faith of death.

Can you imagine sharing a cell with a guy that smoked Spice. That is very seriously dangerous.

There was a guy on one of my wings that was about my age… in his mid - 40s at the time. He was a family man with kids. He was inside for a small credit card fraud. He was only going to spend about 6 months behind the door. So this guy never smoked let alone smoked spice. He was locked in with a kid half his age that was a proper spice head.

The guy told the officer he couldn't handle being in there with a kid that was off his head on Spice 24 hours a day. It was fucking dangerous if nothing else. He was pleading with the officer to find him another cell. The officer said there was nothing free at that time. So the guy just had to live with it.

One night there was loud banging and smashing sounds coming from the man's cell. There clearly must have been a fight going on between him and the spice boy. This was in the evening so we were all banged up at that time. Eventually officers turn up and sort it.

It turns out that the spice boy had experienced some kind of frenzied spice attack. The older guy was asleep when then spice boy jumped on him and started whacking him over the head with a fucking toilet seat. Apparently there was claret (blood) everywhere. Spice boy later declared that he thought that he was hallucinating and that he saw the older man as an intruder that came to steal his belongings.

Spice boy was sent to the block for a couple of weeks. The older guy was left with stitches in his head. He was fuming that the officer that he had previously warned did fuck all to help him earlier when he complained of his fears that things might come out on top if he was left there.

To keep the guy from making a complaint they gave him a single cell for the rest of his stay. I think the guy was quite happy with that result. As I have said earlier sharing a cell with someone else has the potential for serious disaster. If you ever go to prison do what you fucking have to do to get your own cell. Trust me on that one.

Jeffrey Archer

Jeffrey Archer spent 6 months at Wayland prison. Jeffrey Archer is a very famous writer and politician/political analysts. I believe he was there a little while before I arrived. I stayed in about 12 different cells in my 4 years at Wayland and apparently one of the cells I stayed in was the one were Archer spent most of his 6 months. Not too many people can say they have shared a bed with Jeffrey Archer lol!

The Essex Boys Murderer

Jack Whomes, one of the men accused of the 'Essex Boy's Murders' was at Wayland at the time I was there. I only had a brief couple of words with him in the time we were there. This would usually be if we crossed paths whilst walking on the exercise yard.

From what I could see, Jack for the main part kept himself to himself. He didn't appear to mix much with people. The thing that stood out the most was the amount of time Jack spent walking. He was always walking up and down up and down on the yard. When there was exercise time out on the yards there were 2 things that you could bank on happening.

There would be a fight and Jack Whomes would be walking!

Brinks Mat Robber

So I was really getting into the gym at this time, and my physique was becoming quite impressive. Due to 'damaged leg' from the accident I was allowed an additional session per week to help improve my legs strength. This was a special session where only about another 8 to 10 prisoners were allowed into the Gym at that time.

Some lifers also had this privilege if they had a record of good behaviour whilst inside. One of the guys I trained with in these sessions was Kenneth Noye. He was one of the Brinks Mat robbers.

This robbery took place in 1983. £26M of gold, diamonds and cash was stolen. It was the biggest ever British Robbery at the time. The stash that they stole would be worth £100M in today's money

Probably the most famous British heist ever.

Kenneth was a very pleasant, friendly and well-mannered bloke. I bet he had some stories to tell… but I never really asked him anything… we weren't buddies as such but just prison gym acquaintances that met once a week to train in the gym.

It's the Good Life – Living the Dream

In prison you spend most of the time being either bored or depressed but every now and again something happens that puts a smile on your face. At this time I was on E wing. I was on the 2s being the first floor. You could look down to the main landing/association area where most guys would be either playing pool or just doing their thing. I walked out of my cell and Kieran the guy in the cell next to me was looking over and down to the main area.

Inexplicably at the top of his voice, he suddenly starts singing "It's the good life" like he was a tenor at the orchestra to his viewing audience. I started laughing and then joined in. We repeated the words several times at the top of our voices. It got the attention of the whole landing.

Can you believe, we got a round of fucking applause. It was so spontaneous and funny it put everyone in a good mood.

A guy shouts up from the Landing with a smile on his face "What the fuck are you boys so happy about"?

I shout back "We are just living the fucking dream". Everyone cracks up laughing.

The whole thing lasted not much more than 5 minutes but it was something that put a smile on our faces for even the short period of time it was.

The Hustle - Money

Most people have their own little hustle in prison. Some are selling drugs, some coffee and also there used to be tobacco before the ban and canteen shop stuff but I always wondered why people never used stamps as a pay back or currency.

The main reason why inmates hustle in prison is not just to get a better quality of life whilst inside but to somehow make money that will be available to them when they get out.

The only way you can get actual money is by receiving money to a bank account on the outside that is checked by someone on the outside.

This person can then confirm to you over the phone that monies have been received.

However this carries many risks like people bullshitting you that money had been transferred even though it's not showing in your account or being detected by the screws and prison intelligence etc.

Most people ask the buying inmate to repay them in stock from the canteen shop which is not always what they necessarily need or want. You can often see people with 10 bottles of shower gel or 100 chocolates or 50 tins' of sardines and mackerels which they don't need.

Now a stamp in the UK costs around 70 pence. There are some post offices that will bulk buy your stamps off you for maybe a penny cheaper per stamp. You just have to give them some bullshit reason where you got them from. Now for example if you sold £3.50 worth of coffee to an inmate, he then could purchase the coffee using 5 stamps etc etc…

For Example - 1000 stamps = £700.

Cash them in when you get out of prison. A drug deal that costs a man £50….Well he can buy £50 of stamps on the canteen or he can get family to send him stamps. The drug dealer will receive approximately 70 stamps in exchange for the drugs. Not that I would have ever dealt in drugs… that's not me. I did use the stamp exchange theory on a few occasions but not overly but if I wanted to hustle hard on lower ticket items like coffee and other foods whilst inside for those 4 years I could have made £10,000 in stamp 'currency'.

The Hustle - Legal

By now, Inmates were coming up to me for advice on their legal case. These were Guys I didn't even know from other wings in the prison. Word must have got around that I was some kind of legal guru lol!! I did help a few people… but looking at the cases of others I gave them my honest opinion if I thought that had no angle for an appeal. I knew how appeals worked by this stage and had a good understanding of the law. I literally became one of the prisons Jail house lawyer – not officially of course but people would always be asking me questions.

These people had heard about the work that I had put into my own case. This was the on-going hope that I had against the injustice that had been placed upon me. You could often see me writing or carrying around stacks of legal documents. I was relentless. I know now that after this book and the next one which I have already described have been published, that due to the public knowing what I have had to put up with over all these years can assist in finally bringing justice due to the public demand.

They won't get away with it anymore.

The Hustle – Business set up on the outside

I was also now giving advice on setting up a business. Most of these younger guys wanted to set up either a record label or a clothing brand. Now I know fuck all about these industries… so what advice could I give? All I could say was is do their research… and then do more research. Always remember 'cash is king' I said… don't over stretch yourself… don't run before you can walk as such… without money or cash flow you will eventually fuck up.

Mr Pervert

Although there were some right wanker screws, most of us got on with most of them. The female screws were easier to talk to and often more compassionate to the needs of an inmate. This is because I suppose especially for the young ones they were like mother figures.

At my cell door, I was chatting to one of them …. Nothing of great importance as far as I can remember… she looks down the corridor and says "oh look, here comes Mr Pervert"

I laughed "What do you mean Ms" I said… she waited for him to go in his cell and bang up as it was that time of day.

Well after we get banged up, a couple of minutes later and then about 5 minutes after that the officers look through the window flaps on the cell doors to do their counts and make sure everyone is where they should be.

Now you would know which officers were on duty at that time so we would know who would be checking through the cell flap. Apparently what the guy opposite me use to do ('Mr Pervert') was wait for the officers to start checking each cell. You could hear the flaps on neighbouring cells going up and down and knew as the officers would be approaching your cell. Mr Pervert would lay down on his bed and start wanking so that the female officers would see… what a fucker lol!!

Scariest 10 Minutes – were my children alive?

Now I've had some scary moments in my life… being in the middle of shootings even having seen a gun in the my mouth of a guy playing Russian Roulette,…. but I will tell you now, what happened on this particular date in late 2016 was one of the worst.

So I'm in my art class as usual painting my pictures etc just a normal day I suppose. Then in walks one of the priests from the chapel.

Now when a priest comes looking for someone it usually means bad news. Often he has come to report that someone for example has died in your family.

The whole class looks up at him and we are probably all thinking the same thing.

The priest proceeds to ask the art teacher "is Mr Constantinos here"….

"Fuck, fuck, fuck it's me" I thought.

Now when you have lived a life like I have especially losing both my parents in a car accident as you know when I was just 14… you always expect the worse. As far as I was concerned, someone had died and I would automatically think of my children.

I got up… "That's me" I said to the priest 'what's the matter, what's wrong' I said, 'what has happened'

He said he didn't know but I needed to phone my ex-wife urgently. I thought that he must have known and was just keeping it back from me as he didn't want to be the bearer of bad news, but he said again he didn't know.

Now the art room was positioned almost as far away from my wing as you could be… it was the longest walk of my life. I was shaking, banging the corridor walls and making funny noises and shouting....aaaaahhhhhhhh just so that I could get it out of my mind for one split second. I got closer and closer to my wing ..... I think I was starting to lose the plot. Was I about to find out the worst news if my life.

Please don't let it be that one of my children has died!

I got to the wing and went straight to the phone... here we go... I called the ex-wife ... ring ring, ring ring, she answered...

I loudly said "what is it", 'what is it, what's happened, has someone died tell me now'

She was nervy but said "no nobody has died".. Oh my god, that was the biggest relief of my fucking life... "What is it then, just tell me now"......

"Sophia is pregnant" she said.

Well no one wants to hear that their 16 year old daughter being so young was pregnant but in reality at that moment it was the most relieving news that I had ever had.

That was to be my first grandchild. She is almost 6 now.

Whilst walking to the phone my mind was flying with all the possibilities of what I was about to hear. There was something in the back of my mind saying Sophia was pregnant.... Thank God that's what it was.

I tell you that walk from the art room to the phone were the scariest 10 minutes of my life.

Cheese and Jam Celebration
after hearing Sophia was pregnant

Toast, jam and cheese - I have 2 or 3 memories of when I would have been about 2 years old. For some strange reason, one of them was being in the kitchen of the flat that we lived in above my Mums shop. It would have been around 1973.

I was eating toast with jam on and with some slices of cheese by the side of the plate. Growing up and all the way until I was about 45 I thought that a cheese and jam sandwich was a normal thing. I have probably eaten that kind of sandwich more than any other! I do remember as an adult on a couple of occasions that people thought that cheese and jam was a strange mix... however I thought nothing of it and presumed that it was they who were strange in that they had never tried this mix.

So when I was in prison I occasionally ate a cheese and jam sandwich that I would put together... how can you eat cheese and jam together one guy said? Am I the strange one here?

I thought looking back at previous comments I had heard? So I decided to put it to the test. I walked around my wing and asked everyone if they had ever eaten a cheese and Jam sandwich.... No one had... it's me then lol!

So strange that that was one of my first memories and it was strange to everybody else where for over 40 years I thought it was quite normal. Oh well that's how I celebrated becoming a granddad.

Escape

It was a beautiful summer's day. I was working in the gardens at Wayland. I sat down on a bench for a while for a break... t-shirt off...my head was facing the sun... lovely .... Just for those few minutes I could have been anywhere... I felt good....

Then all of a sudden... a swarm of anxious thoughts raced through my mind sending me into a panic attack. My chest tightened… I felt sick… the reason for the panic attack was my on-going case against my confiscation order… this is an order put on you by the government where they ascertain any monies or properties etc you might hold that will be confiscated from you in order to pay back any creditors that I had.

My confiscation order dragged for numerous reasons and prevented me from going to an open prison unless it was paid… If you did not pay your confiscation order you would serve extra time in prison.. in my case maybe another 1 or 2 years… although an order hadn't been placed on me yet at that moment, sitting on the bench in the sun, the panic arose due to me believing that I was going to spend an extra 2 years in prison.

I had a vision I could hear my children calling me "Please get out daddy".…. 'Please get out Daddy'!.

I could hear them, they were close. I got up and started walking around the edges of the garden which were mostly fenced off by the perimeter fencing of the prison. On the other side of the fence was a small forest area… that's where I could hear the voices coming from… I thought my daughters were hiding in there… waiting for me… I couldn't find a way out I started shouting to them to come to the fence I could see them in the forest area… but they never came…

The garden officer took my arm… he must have known something was wrong… all the staff know your medical conditions so that they are aware of circumstances like what just happened to me… I was taken straight to the medical unit… I was there for ages… I don't remember anymore but it appears that I somehow suffered a panic attack, a depression attack and a manic episode all in one go. Fuck me looking back now from what I recall it must have been terrifying!

Due to this attack, I didn't have to work again for 6 weeks. Luckily though, I was in F wing at this time so I had more freedom.

On the Roof

It sounded like they had an army outside due to the guy on the roof - it was night time and I could hear someone jumping around and shouting. It seemed like it was coming from the roof of our building. Other inmates start looking out of their windows. The guys opposite me on another wing were clearly looking in my direction and above me. Someone had climbed onto the roof... officers were standing out in the yard and trying to get him to come down... he wouldn't he was up there for ages messing about.

He was being cheered on by inmates from their cells. Prison officers are not allowed to go up on the roof to grab him or coax him down. It is deemed as too dangerous. Any way this carried on for a while. Eventually he was 'tasered' with some kind of light beam which then enabled them to go and get him... well something like that anyway... I couldn't see as this was happening directly above me... it was a good couple of hour's entertainment though which broke the never ending monotony of being locked up.

Smoking Ban

In February 2018 smoking was banned from prison...this was because a man some years earlier had complained about passive smoke entering his lungs and that he should not be put at danger because of other people smoking… he won! As you can imagine, there were a lot of pissed off smokers in the prison community. For many it was the only treat as such that we had… something to take our mind off things… a few weeks before the ban inmates were stock piling tobacco… if you did still have tobacco at the date of the ban, you were allowed to continue smoking it until it had run out.

Slowly prisoners were running out and that's when the black market moved into gear… 30g pouches of tobacco where exchanges hands for as much as £400… really they were… I know that's ridiculous but some inmates were desperate. As usual the money exchange would happen through external bank transfers.

Although you were allowed to 'vape', certainly at first it wasn't the same…as the tobacco got less and less there was a new trading market opening. That's was in the butts/dog ends of the roll ups! Some people would trade their dinner for 3 or 4 fag butts. They would open these up and put into a new rizla paper and roll up a skinny burn.

For those of you that don't know the word 'Burn' in UK prisons means a roll up or a cigarette.

So now the last of the tobacco was gone and pretty much all previous smokers were now using vapes. The market was now in vape capsules.

Just like tobacco and now with vaping, if you borrowed let's say 'X' amount of tobacco or a vape capsule you would have to pay back between 50% or 100% more which was referred to as double bubble. If you didn't pay it back on the Friday … the day of receipt of your canteen then you could be the victim of 'Black eyed Friday'!

At Deaths Door

You see unfortunately, some people that have been behind the door for so many years eventually lose the will to live and rarely come out of their cell… they have lost any zest for any sort of life and just dwindle away and wait for death.

Worse than Death's Door

One of the worst things that I saw whilst I was inside is a guy that literally had his face melted off. This was a diabolical thing to happen, it was terrible.

Because it is so bad it rarely happens but it does sometimes. You would have to be crazy or really pissed off with someone to do this. Basically you put a load of sugar into a kettle of hot water… mix it about and then through it in someone's face… the boiling sugar sticks to the persons face and burns their skin off… fucking disgraceful.

Mr & Mrs Prisoner and Female Officer

There was some flirting between female officers and prisoners on occasion and could be quite fun, like a relief from the day's monotony.

The female officers were good and controlling the levels of flirting and what was said but it was refreshing as they would give you banter back…officer and inmate romances can happen… my mate in his first prison starting seeing one of the female officers… they got found out and she was sacked… however all these years on, and as far as I'm aware they are still together which is good. You never know in life do you!

My First Steps to Freedom

So I was outside the jail with 2 other guys. One was Bill who was another Essex boy and a smart slightly posh speaking Pakistani guy from North West London who was the same age as me. We are going to call him 'R'.

The freedom I was bestowed was the privilege of being able to work on the grounds of the prison but on the other side of the fencing. In effect I was Free.

The 2 lads showed me what work I had to do. This was mainly picking up cigarette butts from the ground that were left by the chain smoking screws before they entered the smoke free prison.

We would use long metal, clip and grab guns to pick the butts up with, before putting them in a bin bag. I actually enjoyed doing it. I found it quite soothing.

I knew 'R' quite well. He was in the room opposite me on F wing. We seem to have quite a lot in common and started off quite well. However as the weeks went by unfortunately for him he decided to become a bit of a dickhead towards me. I think he knew I was smart and that I had sussed out that he wasn't the person he was making out to be which seemed to have fooled other prisoners, but not me.

I think he begrudged this so decided to start acting like a bit of a wanker.

When I started doing the cigarette clearing with him and Bill outside the prison he started acting like a right fucking knob. Making sarcastic comments and trying to be some kind of clown.

"What's your fucking problem mate" I said…

"What do you mean" he replied…. "I'm only messing about Spyros," 'don't take offence' he said.

I let it go. So it was just the 3 of us at the time that had the privilege of working outside the prison. There was nothing to stop us escaping but you would have to have been stupid to escape... especially as we all only had a few months of our sentence left.

There was a very large shed on the outer grounds that would be like our rest room. Where we could drink our tea and coffee and have lunch. It was full of junk and tools but also had a large white board on the wall. The 3 of us were having a chit chat one day and it was revealed that 'R' had an exceptional knowledge of historical persons and events.

Bill and I would pick a person or a historic event or book and 'R' would give us an exceptional lecture on the matter using the wipe board. We learned about Dante's inferno, Leonardo de Vinci and much more. It was really good.

However, 'R' continued acting in an 'offish' manner towards me. By now I knew why. 'R' suspected that Bill and I were onto him with regards to the bullshit that he used to feed us about his outside life.

He claimed to have been a business man that worked in various fields of finance. He stated that he was in prison due to an investment that went wrong and he was caught on the wrong end of it. This very well could have been true but the rest of his story didn't make sense.

He claimed that he lived in a 3 story townhouse that had an elevator in it just behind Selfridges in Central London. Well such a property in that area could easily cost £10M plus.

If he lived in and owned such a property he would clearly be quite wealthy right?

Well then in that case he could have easily had £25 a week sent into him from his partner outside. On top of that with a prison wage of up to and around £25 per week he could have had £50 per week to spend on the canteen. On the canteen there would be hundreds of products available. These could be from drinks, foods, spices, refrigerator goods, chocolates, toiletries etc etc. with that kind of money you could buy foods where you could cook on F wing… great curries, lasagnes, some really tasty stuff.

Instead of using shitty prison soap, toothbrushes and toothpaste, you could buy better quality stuff.

'R' never ever bought anything. His room was an empty shell. He had nothing. This did not seem likely from someone who was an apparent millionaire.

It became clear in my mind that he was a fake and Bill and I agreed on this.

When we were checked out of reception in the morning before outside work, they would always ask us to confirm our addresses. The address 'R' would give was for a house in Harrow… nowhere near Selfridges. It would have been just a normal house.

It was a town visit day for him. His wife turned up in a car that wasn't the flashy car he said they owned.

His 'wife' showed no emotion or excitement when seeing him.

Through the other clues that Bill and I had identified our confusion was this. He used to live in Harrow with his wife and daughter. They split up.

He then went to live in Leyton (quite a rough part of London) with his parents.

He conducted his crime. He went to prison. He had no money and certainly no big multi million pound house behind Selfridges.

He didn't receive money from family on the outside.

Any money that he earned in prison he saved so that upon his release he would have some money- maybe £2000.

What put the icing on the cake is that he had a confiscation order from what I remember was around £100,000. This was part of the money that he would have possibly earned through his alleged crime. This was money that needed to be paid to the court to allow him to leave at the expiration of his sentence. He did not pay the money and on that basis had to spend another 4 or 5 months in prison.

'R' response to this was that he would rather spend extra time in prison (which meant more time away from his daughter) than pay the £100,000....BULLSHIT!

The reason I have exploited the situation with 'R' was a lesson to him and others. You must be yourself in prison or you will be found out if you talk bullshit. 'R' started becoming a wanker when he knew I had sussed him out. I just wanted to return the feelings to him by including him in my book. Lol. Serve's him right for being a total dickhead.

However having said all of that, I believe that 'R' is a very intelligent guy and has a lot more to offer. I hope to hear some good things about him in the future

Norwich City

So I only had a few months of my sentence left and I had now got to the stage where I would be allowed outside the prison for a family visit. The anticipation and excitement of this was very high. But typical me, due to my anxiety and stresses and mental disorder

I was worried that something would go wrong and it wouldn't happen.

Thankfully it did… the large gate to the entrance of the prison opened and soon after my ex-wife with our 2 daughters and baby granddaughter arrived.

I jumped in the car. I was buzzing… we left the prison and proceeded to drive to Norwich City Centre which was about half an hour away… my girls and I were jumping around in the car singing songs. I had counted hundreds and hundreds of days waiting for this moment.

We got to Norwich and parked the car. The first difference that I saw as we entered the car park was the charging machines for electric cars… That was a bit of a wow moment for me.

Although I hadn't smoked for a year due to the prison ban, I decided to buy a packet of roll up tobacco. I was out for the day and wanted to make the most of it. Walking round the city centre was great… the market stalls were out along with the fast food stalls… I just stood there studying the food rubbing my belly… I think I started off with a Doner Kebab… fucking beautiful.

We carried on hustling around town and 2 hours later it was time to eat again….I'm not sure what the place is called but it was one of those large new style restaurants that serves buffet food… Chinese… Indian… Middle Eastern etc…after 4 years of eating for the most part the same old bland crap this felt like I was in heaven.

It was a wonderful day for all of us. That was my first proper taste of freedom for almost 4 years

The Sue Ryder Charity Shop.

So with about 3 or 4 months left on my sentence I was allowed to work outside the prison starting on the prison grounds but that that wasn't proper out.

The job was to be at a Sue Ryder Charity Shop in the nearest town. I would leave the prison in the morning. I would the cycle about 1.5 miles to the neighbouring small town. Lock the bike up and then it was about a 20minutes bus ride from there to the Sue Ryder Charity shop.

I loved it… I felt relatively free… if I wanted to I could have run off… or called someone to come and get me and I would be off… however I would be on the run…. Not worth it lol with just a few months of my sentence left.

Within that day I would get a couple of Free hours to myself. It was nice walking into shops or having a bite to eat. During the day I was a Free man. However after 5.30pm I was once again a prisoner.

Pushed to the limit

Young guys generally have no children. They believe they have nothing to lose and the life experience of their brains have not developed into anything of substance or knowing as yet.

These 'young ones' are the ones to look out for the most, danger wise. Many of them have big mouths and say and do things that they really shouldn't. They do not appreciate the consequences of their actions etc…. Whereas a 45 year old man for example it is completely the opposite. We have children and responsibilities, mortgages and many of us have wives.

We want to keep our head down and complete our time in peace without some little fuck pissing us off.

There was a young Pakistani boy, only about 20 years old that found it funny calling older blokes 'bacons' (nonces/paedophiles). This guy was really getting on my nerves. However as part of the Muslim Brotherhood that exists in Prison he thought he could get away with it as he would be protected by his 'elders'. He kept making these gestures towards me although he knew full well what my crime was. I went and spoke with his elders. They had a word with him and he stopped.

Some months later I entered into the toilet area in education and there the little bastard was…

"How's it going Mr Bacon" he said. That pushed me over the edge.

I pinned him up against the wall and had my hands around his neck. I was strangling him.

"Say that one more time you little two bob cunt" I said. I was choking him…..someone walked in…."what's going on" he said. I released the boy who then practically ran out of the toilets crying.

That evening I was back in my cell in association time. I had a visit. Two of the Muslim elders had come to see me. I thought the worse but they were very civil on the matter. I told them my version of events. They said they would deal with it. I never knew what they meant by that but the young guy never looked me in the eye again whenever our paths would cross.

The situation infuriates me even more when I consider the criminal injustice that had been placed upon me. I shouldn't have been in prison that long which in effect heightened my chances of problems in prison which could have had further consequences for me.

Another example of the young lads not thinking about consequences was when a Somalian guy only about 25 years old was getting bullied by 3 Pakistani boys over a debt that he apparently owed. The Somalian guy had enough. Once the doors were opened for afternoon work, the Somalian runs over to the other side of the wing.

He steams into the cell of one of the 3 guys. The guy is still lying on his bed. He Jumps on him and starts slashing his face with a shank that he had. Older guys generally would have found a solution but with the young lads they don't give a shit and don't care about consequences.

As I said it's not about walking around like you are a tough guy and getting yourself into risky situations. It's about keeping yourself to yourself' for the most part and getting on with it.

It's not about who the toughest guy is but which guy is willing to carry out the most damage.

How Long Until Bang Up

For anyone that hasn't been to prison but watches programmes on it you will probably think that the dreaded moment each day is when you get banged up for the night usually around 6pm with the door not opening again until 8am the next morning… well actually you would be wrong. When you are floating around in your free time usually between 4pm and 6pm sometimes it is too long. There is often fuck all to do and you pace up and down your wing then up and down again and again wishing the time away. For many inmates, 6pm is a relief!

When that door closes you know where you are with things and you carry on your evening having planned which TV programmes you will be watching and which magazines you will be reading. It is a peaceful time when you can be away from the drug fuelled frenzies that are displayed every evening and away from the dickheads who have nothing good to say.

Hearing that door slam closed for the night can be a relief.

23 Hour Bang Up

23 hour bang up... some people losing the plot - 23 hour bang up can be tough as you would imagine. Imagine being in a room 7ft wide by 11ft long... that's about the same size as a child's small single bedroom for 23 hours without being let out... the room is not packed full of activities for you to do... at best a radio or a TV if you are lucky. Most will have very little food treats.

For many being locked in a room for 23hours non-stop is mental torture. Usually you will find that the younger inmates find it the toughest.

I would say it is physically and mentally unhealthy to cage people for this long. I don't see how prison is supposed to reform you - which by the way is a myth for the most part then how are you going to get better when you are mentally pushed to your limits. It just inspires more hate and confusion.

Prisons to change

Prisons around the world vary dramatically in their appearance, facilities, cleanliness etc. The other day I was watching a documentary on a German prison. I couldn't believe it. It looked like a cross between a spanking new hospital or a school.

The facility was modern, exceptionally clean, decorated to a high level, beautiful paintings on the wall. There are great workshops, basketball, a five a side football pitch, gym and a gentleman's games room that included a pool table and a library. This room didn't look too different than a games room/ library than you would find in a wealthy home! The cells were more like bedrooms. The prisoners all looked calm and happy and understood their sentences, wanted to better themselves…and there were hardly any incidents. They even had a room where they could allow visitors to stay with you for 3 hours per visit…this room would have 2 couches, an eating area, a play area for children and a shower room.

Punishing someone should be to deprive them of freedom. Not to mentally torture them.

Thanks to:

There were some good lads whilst inside… well not good as they allegedly committed crimes but people I got on with.

I had a good select bunch of mates during my time in prison and I just wanted to thank them for making my time easier. I am not in contact with any of them now but would be interested to hear how they are getting on with their lives. These are, 'The Rock', one of the strongest guys I have ever met. He could shoulder lift/ squat over 300kg. He is a seriously powerful guy. We fell out at one stage which was a shame. I missed our football banter. He was a Gooner (Arsenal fan). He was in the cell next to me for quite a while.

Then there was Bruno. This guy was about 6ft 5 inches tall and weighed in at 26 stone! You wouldn't want to fuck with him. He was only about 25 years old when I met him. This guy could push incredible weights in the gym. He really had the potential to become a worldwide renowned strong man. He wanted me to be his manager on the outside after prison and get him sorted into the strongman world. I said I would but again we just seem to have lost contact.

'Steps' was one of the most naturally funny guys I had ever met. He was called Steps because of the way that he walked. This guy could just make anyone laugh with his personality and character. He was also a tough guy though. He weren't scared of anyone or anything. We weren't really that close but we were both Spurs supporters. So we would get together when football banter was going on and take the piss out of the Gooners.

There was Milky…real name Ashley but was named Milky by his mates back in the hood as he was the only white kid on the estate. He was a funny young chap, quite fearless and proper ghetto boy. However you could see a part of him that wasn't a hardened gangster. Would love to know how he is now.

There was also Yardie from Tottenham, Bill another Essex boy, Billy Lee from South East London, Agi a Greek Cypriot guy from Lewisham and a few others. I hope that you are all well boys and are behaving yourselves!

You know I done my time in jail and I ain't ever going back… I say my time…well probably 4 x more than I should have done…if I should have gone to prison at all!

Racism

It must have been around 2004 and Manchester United were' playing Panathinaikos in Greece in a Champions League Game.

We were round my grans in Edmonton. I was listening to a very famous sports station and the presenter that evening was and probably still is that radio stations chief presenter. Anyway he and his guest were discussing the game and who they thought they would win. The chief presenter stated that he thought that the Panathinaikos team were 'better off staying at home and cooking kebabs'

Now that is a very stereotypical and somewhat racist remark… how the fuck did he get away with saying that?

Imagine if United had been for example been playing an African side who he thought had very little chance of beating United. Now imagine this presenter saying that the African team were better off staying at home and cooking a Goat!! There would have been uproar! He probably would have been sacked.

Now here's the thing. Later that year Greece were crowned champions of Europe!, yet the presenter still felt the need to somehow stereotype or racially abuse the Greek side.

I tried to call into the station to have a word with him live on air but I couldn't get through… seems like he got away with it

Racism in Prison

Like everywhere in society there is racism in prison but not quite as you may think. My experience was very different than let's say what you see in American documentaries or films about prison. So from what we see in America the situation appears usually to be as follows.

You are either in a group of blacks, a group of whites or a group of Hispanics/Latin Americans. You will see on the yard that they all stick together and rarely mix with the other ethnic groups. There are strong rivalries between the groups and often gang fights against each other that can end in serious injury or worse.

However in England it appears to be quite different. Although the black inmates on the yard usually hang around in a big group together the rest of the population mix as one. However this does not mean that blacks, whites and Asians (mainly Pakistanis) don't mix together. They do and I did not see at any point any racial tension between the ethnic groups in my whole 4 years in prison. Everyone mixed with everyone quite naturally. For me this would show that mainly black and white relations in the UK appear to be a lot more normal and civil than in America.

Don't get me wrong there are always going to be the odd racists in all groups but nothing you would ever really notice.

I would say that the group of people in prison in England who are the most prominent in their racial feelings and expressions would be working class white people that come from the countryside 'country' not cities. The direction of their racist ignorance or vile would often be against other white Europeans who would be very small ethnic groups within the system.

These smaller European groups would consist of a handful of Turks, Greeks, Bulgarians, Romanian's etc. These smaller groups were in fact not groups as there would only be a few of each race/ country disbursed around the prison. On that basis it would be easy for the racists to single them out.

The racists could not outwardly express their ignorant and dumb arse thoughts against the blacks or Asians as there are far too many of them and they wouldn't get away with it.

In addition it appears that these racists have been brainwashed into thinking that being racist is only when you act wrongly against people of colour!

So being of Greek Cypriot background I literally only met about or 5 other people of Greek Cypriot origin in my whole time being imprisoned. Most if those were only half a Greek Cypriot in any case.

London is my country- I suppose just like in many other western countries the UK I would imagine is quite similar to the USA. In London I am a Londoner…no discrimination that's who and what I am… however am I English?… well that depends on whose opinion you are asking… in London… I am English but of a Greek Cypriot background.

In somewhere like Norfolk… many would not consider me to be English even though I was born in England and have lived here all of my life except for the 7 years I resided in Spain.

Many of those people would consider me to be Greek….

So I was a proper minority and not only that my name was 'Spyros', you can't get more Greek sounding than that.

Here is another example of racism that demonstrates the ignorance of what racism is and can be.

Dumb Arse Country Hillbillies

It's strange. Although I suffered small bouts of racism in prison it wasn't until I got to F wing that it got on top.

So F wing is the best wing in the prison. You have to earn the right to get there. There was about a year to go of my sentence and I was chosen to move to F wing. This wing is more like a large chalet. There were 20 rooms downstairs and 20 rooms upstairs. I was in the very first room on the lower level. The doors are wooden and you have your own keys to your room. Your room had its own shower. This was like paradise compared to where I had just spent the last few years.

Although I had been at Wayland prison for years, there were very few people I knew through that time that had ended up in F wing at the same time as me.

I noticed per capita there were very few ethnic minorities. Most people on that wing were white English people.

The first person that I met was a guy in his 70's. A very bitter looking man that I would soon realise was full of hate against what he perceived to be foreigners.

So this was the time of the 2018 World Cup. F wing had a good size common room with a large flat screen TV. The night that England were' playing their first game,

I sat in the common room with a few others to watch the game. One of them was the old guy that I just mentioned. Soon after these 2 other white guys enter the room. They were sitting to the right of me. I was puffing on my vape machine. So one of the guys turns to me and says

"You know you are not allowed to vape in here" he said. He had a stern face like I had somehow offended him.

"Sorry mate" I said. 'I have seen other people vape in here so I presumed it was ok' I declared.

"What a dickhead" I thought. 'Why did he give a fuck?'

Anyway he then says to me "How comes you are watching the England game…you are Greek aren't you"?

Is this guy being fucking serious I thought. "My family originate from Cyprus but I was born in England" I said –

"Oh so you are Greek then" he said –

"What's your problem mate" I said

So he repeated… "I was just wondering why you are interested in watching the England game if you are Greek"

"Really" I said.

"So what nationality are the players that are playing for England" I said.

He laughed – "Well they are English of course" he said.

"What makes you say that" I said

He said "Well they are white English persons with an English name".

"So why are half the fucking England team black" I said

He froze for a second, didn't know what to say and stormed off.

What an utter 2 bob racist dumb arse wanker.

It appears that the main instigator of the racism was the old guy in his 70s that I just told you about. He would have his small troop of younger white 'country' boys or hillbillies as I used to call them. There was a Romanian guy they picked out and a couple of others here and there. They thought that they were a force in their numbers but I picked each one of them out individually over a period of a few months and fronted them. They all bottled it without their little hillbilly gang members being around them.

On another occasion on F wing there was a chap in his early

20s. We got on well with each other and didn't really mix with some of the people around us…

My name is Spyros not Stavros

On another occasion on F wing there was a chap in his early 20s. We got on well with each other and didn't really mix with some of the people around us…

So one day we are having our usual little chit chat… then out of nowhere he calls me 'Stavros'… which is a stereotypical Greek name, probably made famous by the scene in a Harry Enfield comedy sketch made some 30 years previously. In the sketch Stavros is a kebab shop owner. I never liked the sketch as I thought it gave the impression that Greek Cypriots living in the UK/London were a bit thick or not of the modern times…. Which is totally untrue… indeed per capita people living in England from a Greek Cypriot background have more wealth on average than many other groups of people and are far more likely than most to own their own businesses.

Anyway so I said to the guy… "Why did you call me Stavros"? He, knowing full well that my name was 'Spyros'…. He wasn't sure on what I meant on the matter or that it could be an issue…he said he heard others call me by that… yes but that was by hillbilly racists from 'country'…. 'Country' in our language meant people from rural communities that lived away from major cities where most of the population would be 'White English' people.

I needed to make him understand. This kid was a black guy from London. He needs to understand that racism isn't just about negativity or vile against black people for example.

He still didn't see a problem in it. I don't think that he understood that by him calling me 'Stavros' was in some way being stereotypically racist.

Ok I said "How would you like it if I started calling you 'Winston'….. Winston is a very stereotypical name that is given to a black man in white society. That name was probably made famous by the comedian Jim Davidson again around 40 years earlier.

The guy said he wouldn't care and it made no difference to him….. Even though he knew that Winston was a stereotypical name referring to a black man with a clear essence of racism… So I started calling him Winston… it didn't take long before he got really pissed off and was ready for a fight me!

He calmed down and thought about the situation for a while and realised that calling me 'Stravros' was in effect being racist and only realised when he got agitated and annoyed when I called him 'Winston' that he felt I was being racist.

I think it was a good lesson for him. We were Ok after that. Actually he lived in Dalston right where I grew up when I was a kid. Good lad.

Haters

Do you know what I hate most in life… **HATERS!**

In society we are surrounded by Haters… we'll surprise! There are plenty of them in prison also! The difference is you can't get away from the fuckers!

Haters are generally people that have nothing good to say about anything… if you are in a good mood they will try and put you down… if they are jealous of you then they will try and hate on you…. You will often find that haters are also racist and have come from an unsettling life. They try and infect their own misery onto you. If they are miserable and are suffering then they can only be happy if they can make other people unhappy.

I came across 4 or 5 of these hard core haters in my 4 years inside…. Close to fighting all of them but never happened.

A lot of the jealousy or hatred against me from these guys was because they thought I was smart and had lots of money on the 'out'. Sometimes their banter or hatred got over the top and almost kicked off… wouldn't stop them though. This was their life.

This one guy was a bit of a bully boy and tried it on with me… he would make degrading jokes so I would give it back… one time I was a bit out of order.. I mentioned his religion, priests and children… he pissed me off and pushed me so I retaliated…. Loads of people heard me say it and were waiting for bully boy to react… bully boy looked up at me and said "Say that again and see what happens"…

I said "You heard me the fucking first time so do something now" he did fuck all… what a wanker…. Bullies should be put in solitary confinement. I think a couple of the other lads were thankful as they wanted someone to front him and put him in his place.

I never got into 1 serious fight in my whole 4 years inside – Incredible

One of the most incredible things I found retrospectively about prison was that I never once had a serious fight with anyone. Don't get me wrong there were a good 4 or 5 occasions that it was very close. I had a few minor scuffles on the way but nothing overly. There were a few people jealous of me in prison. It could be that I was smart, had the ability to fight my own legal case, or they would think I had lots of money on the outside. Some were even jealous that I had the ability to flirt with the female screws without going over the top or that I was a good hustler wherein I could always pull off a trade of some kind thinking out of the box.

Grandparents

It was early 2017 my grandmother who had just turned 99 years old passed away. In the later part of 2017 my Granddad passed away just short of 105 years old. These were my dad's parents. My mum's parents had passed away many years before that and at a much younger age.

My dad's parents were in effect and to an extent like my adoptive parents.

It was like losing your parents all over again.

The saddest thing for me is that I had not seen them for a couple of years as I was in prison. They didn't know that. If they had known I was incarcerated I think it would have had a huge mental impact on them.

On that basis the problem I had is that the rest of my family and I had to lie to them as to my whereabouts. We told them that I had gone to work in America as a big job opportunity had arisen for me. I called them from prison sometimes letting them know how I was getting on.

My gran was a little confused by it all and wanted to know how often I was seeing my children. I told her that they had been flown over to America to see me and that occasionally I would fly to England to see them. There were no problems I said and that I would be coming back to live in England soon. She would ask why I hadn't come to see her on my visits back to the UK ....I found excuses.

This was really hard for me... I was lying to them but didn't know what else to do.

Live to 100

I have spent most of my adult life being overweight. I do believe that it is something within our individual genes that makes us fat. However I do also agree that exercise is important to control weight loss but what and how much you eat will ultimately depend on your weight.

However with regards to life span I am sure what you eat has a significant part to play on how long you live.

What I mean is it's not about the bad foods that you may eat, it's about how many good foods or super foods or gut assisting foods that you eat.

I look at my granddad - in my lifetime he was never slim… in fact most of the time he was quite overweight. Now how many overweight people do you see that live to almost 105?

There must be a reason for this. I often watch programmes or documentaries on diets, exercise, super foods, living to an old age etc etc…the common factor that appears to be coming through over the last few years is that many doctors and nutritionists etc believe that living for a long time is not down to the amount of bad foods that you may or may not eat but how many good foods, super foods etc that you eat.

This is because where does your food first go when you eat it? Well we all know that it's your stomach/gut. A good healthy strong gut distributes the nutrients of the food to the appropriate places in the body.

So if you Google what foods provide the greatest anti-oxidants and protection and strengthening of your gut you will see foods such as:

Beetroots, nuts, asparagus, broccoli, blue berries, green leaves and much more.

My granddad use to ear shit loads of this stuff everyday… but he also ate his fair share of bad foods…..

On that basis and in the fact he was almost 105 when he passed away, then sounds quite reasonable that the theory of how much good foods you eat rather than against how many bad foods you eat can have a massive impact on your life span.

My granddad never exercised more than about a 20 minute brisk walk every day.

So get Eating Super foods – that my message

Post Prison

So I had been out of prison for a couple of months now. I initially lived with my ex-wife but then the council helped me find a bed sit in a shared house in the Chelmsford area….

Actually at the other end of the road as to where Chelmsford prison is situated.! Can you believe that… that's the last place I wanted to pass by every day.

So it was a big house. There were 4 other lads in rooms in the upstairs of the house and a couple in the annexe at the back of the house. Luckily I had quite a big room. It was the size of 2 double rooms.

I didn't really mix that much with the other housemates but it was impossible not to bump into them regularly as there were so many of us.

Living with Psycho Jack

There was one guy in the house… his name was Jack… slightly weird character but not overly.

He was only there for a few months then moved out to live with his much older girlfriend that lived over the road.

Anyway it turns out that he split up with her. A few months later he met a girl around his own age. She was from Canada. They would both would had been in their late teens to early 20s.

It turns out Jack was a bit of a psycho. When his new girlfriend decided that she wanted to move back to Canada and would therefore be leaving Jack, he decided to stab her to death.

Poor girl… makes me sick… I think Jack went on the run for a couple of days but was caught up with. He got a life sentence …. I believe he is Chelmsford prison.

Moving out?

So I must have been living at that house for a year when the following happened. I only have a brief recollection of what happened and I don't know why I did it but the reality is I must have been in some kind of manic episode due to my Bi Polar.

I was in the front garden of the house…. One of my house mates came up to me and said "Hi Chris" (I had changed my name to Chris by now…you will see why later) 'I never knew that you were moving out?'

"I'm not" I said….

"Then why have you got all of your stuff here in the front garden" he said …. I'm not sure exactly what I said but it was either that I was selling all my belongings or giving them away.

My house mate couldn't make sense of it and I couldn't understand why he couldn't. He sat me down on the couch which I moved to the front garden myself. He detected that something was obviously wrong. I had previously informed by house mates that I was Bi Polar and it was my duty to do so.

He soon realised that I didn't really know what the fuck I was doing. He helped me move my stuff back to my room. I don't think we ever spoke about it again.

Dating

So after leaving prison, like any heterosexual man I wanted a woman! Lol… I soon started on the dating sites and I had a string of one night stands. After only being out for 2 or 3 months I met a girl that was from Romford. It turns out that her boss at work was good mates with my best man Tim. I actually knew her boss. I had met him on a couple of occasions back in the day when we were younger. The relationship lasted 6 months. I was her first relationship for 13 years which seemed a bit strange. Ultimately though, although she was a lovely girl I believe that she liked her own space and did not want to settle. Looking back we had a nice time but weren't right for each other.

Soon after this I had a fling with another lady. It lasted about a month. She was half Greek Cypriot so we had some common ground but ultimately it turned out to be nothing more than a fling.

My Amazing Grace

I had been out of prison for about a month. It was a sunny day and I got on a bus to Chelmsford. I sat for a while in the High Street. I was just people watching and enjoying the Sun. After a while I moved on to the park which was just down the road. I found my spot near the river. The ducks were swimming and children were playing. The flowers were beaming. I felt really good. It is amazing what a wonderful place the world can be.

I remember looking back on my life and thinking what a waste it has been. The amount of problems that I had caused myself and others was endless.

I knew then that I wanted to be a better person even though I knew much that had happened in my past was not my fault. I had to transform myself somehow. I wanted to give back to society. I wanted to do something meaningful that could have an impact.

I thought about the Angels and the messages that they had conveyed to me. I knew I had to do something. I understood their message.

However - I did not know how to go about achieving this instruction.

Soon after this I met a beautiful lady. We hit it off big time from the first night. She had previously been married for 30 years but her husband left her for someone else. She is an elegant lady that loves horses and has her own stables. At first she was well into me. She made me promise I would never leave her.

So it was going really well with regards to the relationship but at the time with regards to my housing and money and work I started to struggle. In addition she is a very hard working person that is super active and has her life the way she wants it and didn't have the time to spend with me that I wanted. We were together for a year and then drifted apart. However we are still friends and speak every other week. The possibility I believe still exists that maybe in the not too distant future we might get back together again. However if we do not she will always be a friend to me as she helped me in so many ways. I will always be grateful to her....

Being Homeless

I was at Chelmsford bus station. There was a homeless guy floating about. I had seen this guy on numerous occasions over the years… he would shuffle about… I don't think he was more than 35 years old. I don't know how he was keeping alive … he was in a really poor state.

He had no shoes on his feet and the socks that he was wearing were ripped to pieces. I took of my trainers and gave them to him. Probably a few sizes too large for him but for the guy it was like all of his Christmases had come at once.

I got on the bus barefooted and went home.

We live in the UK one of the richest countries in the world… How dare we allow homelessness to still exist? This problem can easily be sorted if the government and its citizens really wanted it to be. It's fucking disgraceful.

I have spent probably about 5 nights sleeping rough in my life. Once was for a couple of nights in around 2013. I was living with

my girlfriend Mel at the time… however we had an argument…
I left her house. I did have a car but nowhere to stay… there were
possibly 1 or 2 family options but I didn't want to put them in the
predicament of allowing me to stay at theirs when I knew for sure
that they wouldn't really want me to.

You would think luckily that I had a car and that would give
me shelter. Unfortunately this could not work for me. You see
I suffer from sleep apnoea which is a condition where you stop
breathing when you are sleeping which wakes you up in a fluster
trying to breathe.

There is a temporary lack of oxygen going to your brain so it
feels like you are going to pass out. The only way realistically I can
prevent it is if I sleep only on my front. This is not possible in a
small car… so unless I wanted to spend the whole night having
apnoea attacks which of course is dangerous for reasons explained
then I would have to sleep outside.

I parked the car in an outdoor car park in Ashford Town Centre
in Kent. I walked around looking for a good spot. I found one by
the bins at the back entrance of Marks and Spencer's.

Job done. The next morning I drove myself back to Chelmsford
and went to the council to try and get some temporary
accommodation. They had nothing close by and wanted to send
me to Harlow or Southend which are miles away.

I got very frustrated and left it… that night I parked by the river
that runs through the city centre. I slept by the river… actually it
must have been a good spot as there were a few other homeless
people there. I went back to the council the next day and was
prepared to take something in Southend or Harlow but luckily for

me they had somewhere a lot closer which was the Oakland Hotel in South Woodham Ferrers.

The other time I slept rough was in late 2021… I couldn't stay around the girlfriends that I had at the time and I couldn't stay around the ex-wife's either for reasons I can't be bothered to explain… once again I done 2 nights by the river. The council then moved me to a 1 star delinquent's hostel in Harlow where I stayed for about a month.

Sleeping rough didn't really bother me as such but there were one or two occasions by the river where I would lie on my side and look at the water in the river. The water made me cry just for a few seconds whilst feeling sorry for myself. I was a 50 year old man. How did I end up in this situation?

It must be terrifying for any female sleeping rough. What kind of 'apparently' 1st world country do we live in that allows women nowadays to sleep rough - Fucking shocking.

On one of these homeless nights I swear down there was a pregnant woman in a small tent about 20ft away from me. What the fuck was she doing out here pregnant I wondered. She started talking with another girl. She said that she had refused temporary accommodation for some reason or another which I couldn't work out. She was drinking alcohol and smoking weed. I don't get it… how could a pregnant woman do that? I wanted to go over and say something to her, but I didn't. It really made me sad.

This reminded me of another situation some years ago. I met a girl on a dating site. I hooked up with her at a pub at Liverpool Street station. We were having a drink or 2 and then cocaine enters into the conversation. She said her made had some… we took a taxi a few miles down the road to either Poplar or Plaistow in East London… I can't remember but it was in some high rise flats…I met her mate… and away we go, the drink was aplenty and we started sniffing the white stuff… but then I couldn't believe it… all 3 of us were bang on it… when my dates mate brought up in the conversation that she was 5 or 6 months pregnant… I was stunned I couldn't believe it… what the fuck is she doing… she has a baby inside her!! I ended up getting in an argument with her and then I fucked off… I felt sick… what a horrible selfish cunt that bird must have been… how could she do that?

So I admit that one or twice over this difficult period, I have taken left over food from fast food shops and cigarette ends from the floor when I had no money. I probably should feel embarrassed by it but I don't really… I had to do what I had to do!

Ancient Alien Theories

For those that remain sceptical as to whether there are beings from other planets and that have visited earth going back billions of years… then they should read more or at least for example watch the Ancient Aliens Documentary series. There are maybe 20 or 30 episodes at a guess. Once you have watched these programmes you will be left in no doubt as to the existence of Aliens. As you will have read I have met 3 of them…**The 3 Angels.**

Star Trek

I was always fascinated by the programme series Star Trek. I believe that the writers were not just having thoughts of the future and places far, far away from earth. The themes, topics and morals that were displayed in each episode I believe were in a way a sort of message what the future could hold.

I fantasise about being similar to a being that I saw on an episode of Star Trek. The being was going through a painful metamorphosis changing slowly into a superior being. His current state of being was killing him but eventually the metamorphosis was complete and he transformed into a bright and shinning golden colour with immense capabilities. He literally was so powerful that he could do anything. He beamed himself off the Star ship enterprise into Space where he would have the freedom to visit new worlds.

I need moments like these where my mind can drift to something that makes me feel happy. Breaking the chain of depression is not easy but when I can be that person in that episode of Star Trek... at least in my mind for a short while then it brings me some form of temporary happiness.

Now 30 or so years ago if you believed in Aliens for example like David Icke you were thought of as being crazy or delusional. However passing time has swayed thought... speak to any intelligent person or scientist now and they will inform you that you would be crazy not to believe in beings from outer space now. In fact it is scientifically quite inconceivable that we are the only living creatures outside of planet worth. Mathematically it does not and cannot make sense otherwise.

The Awakening of the scriptures and prophecy

I started believing initially that I was the Son of a superior alien nation as early as 15 years old. I do not believe I am the direct Son of God but on occasion I have received messages from a superior alien race that have the ability to infiltrate my brain as and when they please.

These being are the 3 Angels that I have already described within this book.

I believe that I am destined soon to reach greater heights of intelligence and continue in a pathway that will help the world with its major problems. I was in effect instructed to write this book in order to start a game changing philosophy to change the world… I believe that this is my destiny. This will be my legacy.

The messages that I have been sent by the 3 angels are clear. The world is not as it should be with regards to the equilibrium of wealth. The extreme distance from the wealthy to the poor is not an acceptable situation and does not follow the pathway that our God wants us to take.

We are after all his children.

If you had 10 children that would grow up under differing circumstances, from being very rich to very poor, then how would you feel about that? The 10 brothers and sisters would all know of each other and how to contact one another. However 2 of 10 of the siblings would be very rich and a couple would be very poor. The wealthier siblings could easily help the poor ones. However, they did nothing or very little to help them. Would you not be saddened that your children would not help each other? Of course you would. So how do you think God feels when he looks at us on earth? We are all brothers and sisters that have evolved from the creation of God.

So why doesn't God directly help the poor and needy?

Free Will

How can there be a loving God unless he has given us Free Will? Well there cannot be.

Giving us Free Will is the greatest gift that we could have been provided with. Think about it just for a second. If God did not give us Free Will then he would have created life but in the form of a robot or even a slave. Would you want your kids to be born into a world where there are no choices, no good or bad, no challenges, only love and where there can be no hate? Firstly it simply wouldn't work and secondly having no Free Will has an essence of evil.

Therefore on the basis that god has given us Free Will, he will not intervene as we must as intelligent beings create our own destiny's and what will be will be.

Christopher Hitchens

Christopher Hitchens was a brilliant writer and atheist. UK born he immigrated to America in about 1980. He was a Scholar, a writer of many major world topics. Many of his writings and speeches at lectures would surround his beliefs that there can be no God and if there was a God that the God might be evil?

"Why would God allow millions of babies to starve to death due to no food etc"….he would say.

So If God gave us Free Will then why is it questioned that it is he who is to blame for allowing poverty to still be what it is?

Well it is not God who is to blame. It is those of us who have the ability to stop poverty that have Free Will that are to blame. The reason that babies starve to death is the fault of their wealthy brothers and sisters from within the human population on earth who have not chosen the Free Will and love that God has given to us to help others.

There is enough money in the world to stop poverty. That is a fact. However it is the greed of the wealthy that is preventing the cure taking place.

Evil is that which is morally wrong or sinful; it can also be defined as the absence of good. Since God is good and the measure of goodness, evil is essentially that which goes against His nature and His ways. Evil exists in our world because some of God's creatures rebelled and continue to rebel against Him.

Therefore we all know from the love of god it is good no help others but some remain masked against god and in effect are rebelling against him as they allow evil to overcome themselves by not helping others.

I believe that there is confusion in the world as to exactly who or what god is.

I believe that God exists in everything and everyone. God is a spiritual being of sort that we cannot directly see and is so powerful I do not believe our minds are anywhere close to being able to understand how God created itself and then the multiple universes that I know exist.

God is so far, far far beyond our capabilities of understanding that even if the human race existed for another million years and our intelligence expanded so vastly that we will still not be able to understand how God came to be.

However through influence, direction and evolution going back millions and millions of years the fundamentals of God are installed within all of us.

This on-going installation of knowledge of what God is and what he wants from all of his children is to have love and to have Free Will.

There is only 1 God

Going back thousands of years there have been around 1000 Gods that have been depicted in writings from China to India to the Middle East to Africa and Europe and beyond....

But hold on a minute there is only 1 God ...right? Yes that is right. So if there is only 1 God then who are the other 999 beings that through our recent human history have been depicted as Gods.... And if do they exist... well there can't be 1000 Gods right? .... That doesn't make sense.

Well as just stated there is only one God... but guess what, these other 999 beings that have been perceived as Gods do or did actually exist also.

But they are not gods.

They are superior beings that come from all corners of the universe that over millions if not billions of years have visited planet earth.

They are in effect superior Aliens.

I'm pretty sure that most of us would believe that they were some kind of superior being.

However if we go back a few thousand years to Ancient Greek or Ancient Roman times, their education and knowledge of the world and universes would have been on a significantly lower lever than it is now. Therefore their understanding of the perceived miracles that they saw then must have been God!

So yes these other 999 Gods existed/exist but they in actual fact are not Gods at all but just random superior beings from far, far away that have visited earth.

Some people say … oh well I have never seen an alien… or why don't they show themselves… well the clear answer is they have… these aliens have been noted in scriptures going back thousands by persons covering all corners of the earth that had no contact with some other parts of the earth back then.

If you were to look into the sky now and see the figure of let's say a human being riding a chariot with flames, large beams bursting out and travelling at incompressible speeds…. Would you believe that it was a) a superior alien being or b) God?

What is the main message of the Bible and other Old Scriptures

The main message of the Bible is that God is restoring the world to His original design through Jesus Christ.

The world is in a state of brokenness because of mankind's rejection of God and His plan. Jesus entered into a broken and hurting world to die on the cross to restore mankind to God.

God gave us free will when He created us, which enabled the possibility of sin. We all are given the free choice to do Good or to do evil. God didn't create us as robots that were programmed to do his will.

He chose to give us free will to freely choose to worship, love, and know Him

He created people out of love for the purpose of sharing love. People were created to love God and each other. Additionally, when God created people, he gave them good work to do so that they might experience God's goodness and reflect his image in the way they care for the world and for each other.

KINGDOM FORFEITED: Man rejected God's will and plan and went his own way (Gen. 3:6-7). This is what the Bible calls sin. Sin is when we depart from God's plan and go our own way. Sin is what leads us to brokenness (Rom. 3:23). This result's in death entering into the world (Rom. 6:23). God created a perfect world without brokenness (Gen. 1:31). Man opened the door to sin and death, leading into brokenness.

We must listen to our women as they are the Holy Grail.

Have you noticed how many Flowers and women's vaginas look similar … this is a gift to the earth to remind us of the beauty of femininity… most of the world has plenty of flowers and is a message to us for a reason… the beauty of the world comes in a feminine form and to remind us that the greater of the parts of good come from femininity.

Indeed in Leonardo de Vinci's painting – The Last Supper, we can see with closer inspection the V shape sign that separates Jesus and one of his disciples or indeed Mary Magdalene? For it is a vision that the V representing the woman and Mary Magdalene which are the Holy grail of immortal life.

I believe that the 3 angels that have visited me provided me with a vision on not only how we must look after females but we should as beings take more notice from them with regards to the future of mankind. I believe that women are closer to God than men are and are therefore better positioned in fulfilling Gods plan.

I believe that there is only one fundamental thing in life which is not governed by Free Will and that is love.

I like others think that the nature of love makes it incompatible with a certain type of freedom.

Therefore if love cannot be free will as it is a direct component of what god is then we cannot choose who we love.

If that is so then whether a man loves another man or a woman is part of the evolution of life and how it has developed itself through the will of God.

Homosexuality cannot be Free Will it can only be Love

For those religious people that believe in God and all of his creations who then apparently condemn homosexuality…. Well this doesn't make sense.

God created life in the beginning… I have already stated that this could have been hundreds of billions of years ago. He created life knowing that it would evolve in its own way and time.

He knew the incredible possibilities and diversities that he was creating would produce an infinite amount of possible life forms which could intrinsically be wrapped with in each other that create all or unlimited forms of life. I have already established that any true good or great God could not or would not have created anything different as life has to be Free will and evolve into what it will be.

From the age of about 3 we knew our nephew was going to be gay… he was effeminate, camp and enjoyed playing with dolls…. why was he acting like this! Well that's easy… it was natural to him… normal… his brain didn't know anything different which means in effect he was born gay.

So fundamentally what is the difference between a man and a woman beyond the way we look. Well it's the way we think. A woman's mind is very much different to a man's. The chemistry that works in a woman's mind is different to that of a man's. The chemistry of what they find attractive is also different to that of a man.

Therefor if a baby is born male but through the evolution of life and free will, it is quite conceivable that a portion that are born may have an overriding female chemical make-up within their genes or their DNA that makes them think emotionally and sexually like a woman and Vice Versa.

This is the creation of God in that he created life with the ability to have its own free will and adapt and evolve naturally without an on-going input from God himself. That is the greatness of his creation.

Therefore if those religious entities that believe that homosexuality is not permitted or has not been allowed through his creation then you are wrong and cannot truly understand the word of God with regards to love and free will.

Love is not a choice... it is embedded within us. Love is not part of Free Will for if we are the children of god then we must have love. Anything else thereafter is the Free Will of a being.

Therefore if love is not a choice but is the fundamental and imperative part of God's being then that part of being is not Free Will. Therefore if Love is not Free Will then a homosexual person born with mixed sexual genes will love accordingly to those genes.

I am the messenger

I am not a prophet as such but just for whatever reason have been chosen from birth to remind people of the scriptures that the great prophets of the past have already detailed to us.

I do not change or indeed I have not been instructed to change the previous writings within the great scriptures of our past. My words are just to remind the people of parts of the old writings with regards to looking after our brothers and sisters of this world.

These are the poor and the needy.

The Third Encounter with the 3 Angels of God

I believe the suffering I have been through has allowed me to understand God. I don't believe I would have been chosen by the 3 angels without this suffering.

It was in the summer of 2022 that I last had a visit from the 3 alien angels. I was in the garden of my bungalow clearing up some branches and small twigs that had fallen from my apple tree. My back was facing the front entrance to the garden. I felt a swooping gust of wind enter my back. It was a beautiful tingly feeling that sent shivers down my spine.

I knew that there was something going on behind me…. I turned and there they were', the 3 x 8ft tall feminine angels that I had seen I believe twice before. They were looking at me and their eyes drew me forward to them.

Towering above me, one of them put their hand on my shoulder, and another their hand on my other shoulder with the last one putting her hand on top of my head. I had a profound feeling of happiness so strong that I do not believe that I have ever had such a feeling before.

They were talking to me but not through their mouths but through their hands. I was in a state of ecstatic motionless. Once again I could see colours that I had never seen before and a complex matrix system of the brightest white lights shooting in different directions. They were once again showing me the future. The future holds infinite possibilities of all the possible life forms and what can become in the futures of those life forms

The message was clear… we have the choice in effect in this life as to where we go to in the next life.

However this world is unbalanced and not how God wanted us to be.

He wants his children being all of us, to be like brothers and sisters and to not allow others to suffer when we can help them. I saw scriptures and I understood that I was being chosen to write this book. Then from there show a pathway to the true Glory of God where others would follow and help where possible to change the imbalance that exists on our planet. I don't know for sure how long our meeting lasted…. But … whoosh….. The 3 Angels were gone again.

Curing Poverty

Can we actually achieve this goal? Yes. To end extreme poverty worldwide in 20 years, economist Jeffrey Sachs calculated that the total cost per year would be about $175 billion.

This represents less than one per cent of the combined income of the richest countries in the world.

Billionaires Death Row

How many billionaires would it take to end poverty?

"If the top 500 billionaires in the world pooled the increase in their net worth from one year, they could eliminate extreme poverty seven times over."

2. "... and those who hoard up gold and silver and do not spend in the way of Allah, announce to them a painful punishment, on the day when it shall be heated in the fire of hell, and their foreheads and their sides and their backs shall be branded with it. This is what hoarded for yourselves, so now taste what you hoarded" (Ch 9:33-34)

Shark Tank Money

Although I like programmes like Shark Tank and Dragons Den... some of the guys on it (being the Dragons or the Sharks) really piss me off sometimes. Their love for money thing comes across that it is the only love in their life. Their desire for more and more is ok but only if they use it well.

A few years ago I was reading how a so called philanthropical billionaire gave away £35M to charity in one particular year and that a big thing was being made of it due to his so called generosity.

Is that a fucking joke? How does giving away £35M in one year to charity when you are a billionaire represent philanthropy? I would say giving away £500M plus would be philanthropy. Why not do that?

What the fuck do they need that extra £500M for? Is it to pointlessly purchase another Super Yacht or an Aeroplane?

Image there are about 2700 billionaires in the world. Now imagine they all gave £500M each to good causes like poverty or orphaned children. That equates to £1.5 Trillion! Imagine how that money could be used to stop poverty and give orphans a better chance in life.

This is one of the reasons I do not like the world we live in.

How can you have people that are filthy rich and then some mothers who watch their babies die because there is no food to feed to them.

Poverty is also a preset to crime. Curing poverty reduces crime

Therefore when I state to you that the curing of poverty can widely stop crime then it makes sense. So the guys on Billioanire's Death Row will have a lot to answer to as it is their Free Will which has allowed them to Sin and act with evil. Therefore it's is the fault of these Billionaires that there remains poverty and entail crime.

My Life Now

Why did I change my name - in 2021 I changed my name by deed poll from Spyros Constantinos to Chris Constantino. If you Google my birth name then you will see various newspaper articles about my alleged crimes. This will hinder me for the rest of my life. It is unfair that I should be ridiculed in these articles without people knowing the whole truth as to what happened and more importantly why things happened as they did.

I should not have to carry the burden of this false information for the rest of my life. So on that basis I felt that I needed to change my name. Close friends and family still call me Spyros. However for everything else my name is Chris. For the moment that's just the way it has to be.

It's been a struggle since I left prison. Just imagine spending 4 years inside not even knowing if you did anything wrong. If I had a fair trial and was still found guilty there is no way I would have spent more than 1 year in a Category C prison let alone 4. The main problem for me whilst imprisoned was the last couple of years. My Bi-polar mind was struggling daily and I was being mentally tortured.

Where I was outgoing before prison, I am now turning into a bit of a recluse. I don't like going out and really only go out if I have to. I am an alcoholic and I use alcohol to try and bring some temporary lifting or buzz to my mind to take me out of my monotonous and slightly depressive daily regime.

My probation period ends at the end of June 2023. I believe it will be healthy for me to spend some time in Cyprus near the sea. The sea for me is one of the most wonderful things in the world. Being in clear sea water, slightly chilled gives me as greater feeling as any that exists in life. I need to be more active and being by the sea can provide me with this need.

I live in a small bungalow on the edge of town. Only a few miles from where my children and 3 grandchildren live, that is great. I rarely go out as I don't for the most part like facing other people.

Luckily I have not snorted cocaine for a few years now… but I do still drink a lot of alcohol… my life is quite lonely… and I don't know if it is appropriate for me to try and find a girlfriend as I cannot predict my future with regards to my mental illness.

Recently, I was queuing at the cash machine in town and there was a girl ahead of me. She seemed a bit fidgety and was talking fast gibberish. She got her cash out and turned to me…

"I need the money because I have to go shopping but I don't know where"… 'I must keep walking' she said…'it's my bi polar' she said …. 'I've got to keep going, bye'… and she moved on fast paced down the road. She was clearly on a manic episode. It's the first time I believe that I had seen another bi polar sufferer in a manic episode. I didn't know what to do…. As she carried on steaming down the street I shouted out 'be careful'.

I love programmes and documentaries about serial killers. Not that I like what they did… I'm not an animal but i find the complexities and puzzles that are left for detectives that try and catch these evil perpetrators intriguing.

I can think out of the box and believe that I can see clues or possibilities where others can't.

I have watched many of these real life documentaries over the years. The programmes would detail the investigations and let's say half way through the investigation, I will have worked out what they need to do to catch the killer.

On 2 or 3 occasions I have been proven to be right. In effect that by the time they have got to the end of the investigation which could have been achieved months or years after I realised what they had to do to catch the killer, the same methods were ultimately used as I would have done to catch the killer. In effect what I am saying is that bad I have been part of the investigation team the killer would have been caught much earlier… my mind can see through complex plans and strategies very fast and effectively… hey maybe in a different life I could have been a detective!

Ann has to put up with my problems for many years… certainly since we parted in 2007. I have always tried to help her and the kids as best I can. However the kids and I should be very thankful to her for what she has done for them over time.

A question is often asked… if you could change something in your life and go back what would you change? You will find that most people are apparently quite happy in their lives and wouldn't change a thing

Well, apart from having my daughters I would Fucking change everything that's happened since the age of 14… overall it's been pretty disastrous.

I often dream about my mum and dad… mostly my dad but unfortunately for me the dreams aren't good. My dad was a good man… brought me up well and I respected him… I have great memories of both my parents as a child and no bad ones.

However my dreams have decided to see my dad in a different light… they are usually the same kind of dreams but appear to have got worse and not better over time.

They started off many years ago as if both my parents were sort of strangers to me and my dad was sort of ignoring me or didn't want anything to do with me. These dreams progressed to the point that my parents didn't actually die in the accident but decided after it they wanted to split up and go their own ways… neither wanting the responsibility of looking after me or my sister anymore so that's why we were left to relatives.

In my dreams I would question to my grandmother, what really happened and then one time… actually the first time of many dreams thereafter my grandmother would tell me it was true… that they were alive but went their own separate ways… this is an on-going and quite frequent dream I have… I wish it wouldn't happen… what a way to spend possibly the rest of my life thinking about my parents when I am in a dream state!

My sister and I would often joke when something bad happened to us that has been was quite often that 'we thought that it was going to be easy' this was a reference to our life which came from when I first had this thought. I was about 16 years old and in my small house in Edmonton …North London. I was sat there thinking what kind of a life was I going to have considering the loss of my parents a year or so earlier. I came to the conclusion that I must expect a great life as a great life would be the compensation I would receive for losing my parents at aged 14… 'I thought it was going to be easy'… oh dear got that one wrong then!

So as I said my sister has obviously had a fair share of bad luck or bad things happening to her.

She was engaged to a guy that she met some years earlier that coincidentally lived just down the road. They had a son and things were going great for her. However she found out that her fiancée was having an affair with his ex. My sister was devastated and I believe at one stage she felt suicidal. I was in prison when this was all happening. I was gutted and angered by the situation but there was nothing I could do to comfort her being inside.

Her fiancées parents were very angry with him and to an extent sided with my sister. My sister got on well with his parents and as they literally only lived around the corner, her 'father in law' would pop round to the house sometimes during the day whilst my sister was at work, to see if there was anything that needed doing.

Well ok that seemed fine.

Anyway… one time my sister came home from work … went up to the bathroom and noticed which she believed that she had previously noticed, that her toothbrush seemed to be quite dirty. This was strange as my sister is very clean and would not allow her toothbrush to be so dirty. Something weird was going on.

She discussed it with her cousin who is like her older sister who also lived locally to her.

Anyway they set up a camera on the landing as they suspected someone might be coming into the house and messing around with her stuff.

The camera was set up. My sister would check the camera each night. On this particular night the camera caught someone in the house! It was her 'father in law' ….anyway to cut this disgusting story short…

it appears that her 'father in law' would on occasion when entering the house stick my sisters toothbrush up his arse and was also caught on cameras masturbating over a pair of my sisters knickers… Filthy horrible scum bag…

This was obviously very upsetting for my sister. It was reported to the police who arrested the man… he was eventually sent to Pentonville Prison for a few months. His wife never left him… why the fuck would she want to stay with a disgusting wanker like that… fucking shocking.

Spirit of Mum

Ghost of mum - my sister who now has a son that is 8 years old at the time of writing was shocked one morning. Dino walked out of his bedroom and saw a lady standing before him in the hallway. Dino is a very smart and astute boy and if he says he saw someone then he did.

He told my sister and she did not know what to make of it. There was definitely no one else in the house.

A few months later my cousin Peter saw a spiritualist you know a psychic. Peter and my sister are like brother and sister themselves as my sister spent much of her time living with him as kids after our parents died in the car accident.

Peter did not know anything about the events that took place a few months earlier with Dino seeing someone in the house.

Whilst with the psychic, she felt a presence. The presence was that of an older lady. The psychic told Peter that this lady was telling Peter to apologise to his nephew for shocking him at the house.

Now Peter only has 1 nephew on our side of the family and that is Dino.

Peter called my sister to let her know what had happened. My sister confirmed the incident that took place some weeks earlier.

They were clearly both shocked. The evidence does clearly suggest that Dino was visited by a spirit on that day and that spirit must have been my mum.

I have been visited by Angels and this is a fact that I believe that I have evidenced but I think that what happened with Dino is clear evidence that there is a spirit world out there which further evidences the words of the Angels.

Having a laugh

I suppose one of the things that I look forward to is when my 2 wonderful cleaning ladies come over every couple of weeks to help me do some cleaning around the bungalow. Cherie and Tilly that are sisters, are a bundle of joy and there is great banter between us. That puts a smile on my face for an hour or two as it can be funny with the banter and allows me to speak to people face to face which I don't often do these days.

Andrew and Peter

I have always had a good relationship with many of my cousins. Andrew's mum and my mum were close as sisters. I have a lot in common with Andrew. He has also had his own share of problems over the years. One of those problems was drinking. However at the time of writing he has been tea total for over 2 months now. I speak with him most days as we try to guide each other to a better life by understanding our daily activities and thoughts. This has helped me a lot.

Peter has always been the sensible one out of my cousins. He has done quite well for himself and always helped me whenever possible.

I have learned how to cook better meals and I enjoy this. Since I started painting in prison I have realised that this is something I really enjoy. I am going to start again soon but I am waiting until I have more money to buy all of the materials that I need. It's not that I am a good painter but it gives me a feeling of freedom and peace.

Greek Music

When you listen to a slow English language love song/ sad love song there is no feeling or method of dance that an individual can interpret to body movements of dance that reflect the words of that song.

However with Greek dancing I find it very different. A sad love song could be playing for example and a man can dance by himself and in front of a crowd in a unique slow but moving may. Each movement grips the words of the song in such a powerful way. It is like theatre. It is so powerful.

There are very few things that can make me cry. You supposedly cry in your first night in prison. I didn't but for some reason when I listen to some certain Greek songs the tears come flooding out.

Even as a young child and being at Greek weddings, listening to some of the songs make me feel very emotional. I have tried to put my finger on why I cry so easily when some Greek songs are playing.

The UK makes the best songs that have ever been written.

However I don't believe I have ever listened to a song sung in English that has made me cry.

Greek songs are so powerful and the words are overwhelmingly deep and profound that just hit you right in the heart. It is like your emotions lose control. I find that Greek music and songs often have a feeling of poverty to them. This creates a very sad vibe. The songs are often about love like most songs but they are so sad they just put tears in your eyes. The songs feel like they could have been written by poets hundreds of years ago rather than the modern day swag of UK pop songs.

Remorse

Do I feel remorse about what has happened in my life… of course I bloody do!

I set a wine investment company at the peak of when it was making the most money in its 300 year history. As far as I was concerned at the time I was making my clients money and these clients would be so happy that they would stay with me for life.

Instead my bi polar in effect fucked it all up.… I got sent to prison and stayed there a lot longer than I should have done and that in itself, almost cost me my life.

I lost a lot of money for a lot of people who in many instances could not afford to lose that money. I am very sorry for that and I can assure you this does not sit well with me at all and will forever torture my mind.

My kids missed out on 4 years of being with their dad and many of my family consider me to be slightly mad or insane.

However it's not my fault that part of my skull was cracked in the car accident when I was just 14 years old and it's not my fault I have been infected with Bi Polar disorder due most likely to have been from the effect of losing my parents at such a young stage.

However, I do once again provide a sincere apology to all those that have been affected by me.

The end game

You know, I now don't want much in life.… I really don't… I just want to be happy as I do not understand nor does my brain allow me to have that emotion for any period longer than a few minutes. It is a terrible mental disease with the depression and inability to know what is left for me in my life.

The only genuine thing that I believe could make me happy is to help other people who are in need. This is mainly orphans or people living in poverty or people with mental illness.

I can see no other purpose in my life other than that.

I would be happy to live in a small home right by the sea, maybe on a Greek island or Cyprus. I like to paint to cook and to swim in the sea. If I could live out my years doing that I believe that it would make me happy.

Giving Back

The messages that I have received from the 3 Angels is to promote awareness to the Rich people around the world for them to use a much larger amount of their wealth to help the poor and needy.

I was chosen from birth and have been slowly guided into this direction. I was able to sell face to face like no other. I have suffered so I understand what it is like to suffer. I am smart. I have turned over millions of pounds. I have been close to death on several occasions. I have seen the good, the bad and the ugly that life has to offer.

I have found my own Amazing Grace within the contacts with the 3 Angels. They have shown me the light and the way and the future of what needs to be done. They have chosen me to fulfil the prophecies with regards to poverty.

Using funds from the sales of this book, any future books and any films to be made, it is my objective and instruction to start generating through my foundation, a greater level of awareness to the very wealthy so that they return to the Love of God and use their wealth as they should be. For their wealth does not belong to them, it belongs to God.

Yet for many they have decided otherwise

Although my bi polar disorder prevents me from wanting to mix with other people these days I still feel that if there was good cause for it I could stand in front of 2000 people at a seminar for example and discuss my views on certain things happening around the world which are not right.

To those Billionaires – I am coming for you – I can out think you and can out philosophise you – Please be ready for me. Please be ready to save the world.

I will then also explore various possibilities where I can directly help those in need. I wouldn't just donate the money direct to existing major charities because I want my readers and I to be fully aware of exactly where the money will be going to and who and how it will be helping them.

That's why you will note that I am requesting your contact details as a reader. This is so that you can be informed of how much money has been made from sales of this book and any other things like documentaries or a film that are produced on the basis of my book and then how much of the money will be on-going put into the foundation.

You will individually receive yearly reports on where your money has been used.

I sometimes think what my life would have been like with parents. It's been a very long time since I have had parents. I sometimes wonder what is must be like to have them and how my life could have been very different….what would I be doing now, how my life would have panned out.

When I look back upon my life it's usually with a sense of shame but I don't think I have always been the one to blame…my mind operates in a certain way due to my bi polar disorder. What others may see as wrong or crazy is often the opposite for me. I can only do what my mind tells me is right and what is wrong. On that basis I do not believe I knowingly did anything wrong at the time of running the businesses.

The last message that I had was telling me to write this book. I believe that my messages are being sent to various people around the world at the moment… It's last chance once again for us. The world is not heading in the right direction even though man now has the intelligence to know what is right and wrong.

A world with continued poverty and divide from the rich and the poor cannot exist. There will eventually be an internal explosion of anarchy that will destroy the world.

Evil will over-come good unless people are given the opportunity to live a life without fear, hunger and struggle. I repeat there is enough money in this world to stop poverty.

That is what God wants his children to do now.

I used to look at myself in the mirror and fear I would see the face of the devil after those disgraceful nights out.

When I see women with kids stealing from shops it makes me sad and happy at the same time - why should any woman anywhere in the world have to worry about feeding her kids….

Imagine what that must be like.

10. "Some are born great, some achieve greatness, and some have greatness thrust upon them" … This line is from the famous play of Twelfth Night,

…..let us see what greatness can be achieved through my reminders of the prophecies and my foundation to help the poor and the needy.

Redemption - My on-going fight for justice

I have now spent over 7 years personally fighting for justice for my case. You will have read earlier on within the book how I was let down by my defence solicitors and QC before trial and during trial. I absolutely on many counts did not have a fair trial. A fair trial in the UK is 'absolute' and any verdict taken without all relevant information being evidenced at trial cannot stand.

I have completely evidenced that I did not have a fair trial and that had I received a fair trial then I certainly would have received a much lesser sentence or no sentence at all or not have been found guilty.

The fact is that these 3 verdicts are clearly all possible due to my Bi Polar condition along with potential brain damage, being at high risk of suicide and having alcohol and drug problems during the alleged time of the offences. This makes my sentence repugnant not only to the court but also to the common man and especially to those with mental illness.

Over the last 7 years I have been let down by solicitors, QC, court of appeal, judges and the Legal aid authority who have all chosen to turn a blind eye to my appeals and simply in effect copy and paste the proven negligence and lies committed by the trial defence counsel. Their errors are so blatant and so profound that there is no real possibility of negligence on their behalf. The only possible conclusion which is evident is that they have all acted criminally in order to protect the 'Brotherhood' within the justice system.

They thought that they might get away with it but they won't. In my next book due to be published in early 2024 you will read all of the evidence that will clearly leave you in no doubt that I have been subjected to corruption. Indeed the book I believe at this stage will be called '**Corruption within the UK Justice System.**

No person or authority will be left unscathed by what you will read.

I spent 4 years in prison for an alleged crime I did not know I was committing. In fact if you look at my story then what crime did I actually commit knowingly?

I suffer with bi polar disorder that includes psychosis and have now been on medication for this for 10 years. All of the traits and characteristics of bi polar have a complete nexus with how the businesses were run. I acted with delusion, grandiosity, was gullible and led down the garden path by others.

I received messages from Alien forces before I even met the 3 Angels that it was my duty to stop poverty in the world. I was the chosen one, someone who could do no wrong and at each phase of the failing of the business I was determined and sure that it was all going to end okay.

On the basis that my thoughts were I was doing the right thing at all times then I cannot be guilty of the alleged crime.

Instead though I was left mentally tortured for all the reasons I have already explained to you within my book.

I do not want the UK justice system and it components to get away with what could have ended up in effect as manslaughter if my suicide attempt in 2017 been successful.

I believe that the main reason that I have been denied justice is that the components of the justice system thought that they could get away with it as it was me personally fighting the case and they therefore could swerve the issues and no one would know any better of it.

I could not use a solicitor to fight my appeal as I had no money for the appeal. I was not granted Legal Aid by the Legal Aid authority so that has left me where I am now.

However the Legal Ombudsman have not refuted that I have a claim for poor service provided against my trial solicitor and QC but they have determined although I believe unfairly that I am time barred to make a claim against them. I am however not time barred to make a complaint against the Legal Aid Authority and intend to do so later in 2023 when I receive more support that will be generated from the impact of this book.

I want legal redemption and I am sure it will happen.

Conviction quashed - I would like help getting my conviction quashed as legally that is the only correct option.

I want the legal people brought to justice - ultimately as part of my redemption I need to know that those legal providers that have acted negligently or 'worse' will be brought to justice. It cannot be allowed for them to get away with such blatant and scandalous acts which almost cost me my life. Indeed if they are not exposed then what?

Might this happen again to someone else? I say it is very possible.

I studied and learnt law not just for my sake but for others. I have spent 7 years studying law and working on my case. There is clearly corruption within the UK justice system.

Benediction

My final Benediction is that the world wakes up to the word of God. For those that are wealthy and to continue the sin and rebellion against God then they have chosen evil.

I want the world to read the book - I believe that my book is relevant to every human being.

Ultimately not only because my life has been interesting and there is a lot that all kinds of people from all walks of life can learn from but also due to my meeting with the 3 Angels.

Through what appears to be their magical powers or superior abilities they have connected with me and provided a clear insight into the matrix of the various universes but also the need for mankind to start looking after one another.

This was the most significant message that I received. In effect there is enough wealth in the world today to cure poverty. Poverty is also a preset to crime. Those that are in a financial position to cure poverty must do so as this is the word of God.

We are the sons and daughters of God and therefore we are all brothers and sisters. Do not idly sit back and watch your siblings suffer while you bathe in a fake and evil glory of selfishness and with no love.

You have been reminded. You have Free Will. The choice is yours on what you do next. You will reap in the next life what you have sowed in this one. Tik Tok…Tik Tok… Tik Tok

What we do now echoes in your eternity
You must make sure or at least try to
end your faults before you die

I write the book,
I am the book,
the book never ends
There is no genius without
a touch of madness
Tik Tok… Tik Tok… Tik Tok

www.ingramcontent.com/pod-product-compliance
Lightning Source LLC
Chambersburg PA
CBHW021240060726

47590CB00005B/1840